Table of Contents

W9-CYH-291

Table of Contents *(cont.)*

Using
Biographies
in Your Classroom

Author

Garth Sundem, M.M.

Editor Wendy Conklin, M.A.	**Editorial Manager** Gisela Lee, M.A.
Assistant Editor Torrey Maloof	**Creative Director** Lee Aucoin
Editorial Assistant Kathryn R. Kiley	**Cover Designer** Neri Garcia
Editorial Director Emily R. Smith, M.A.Ed.	**Cover Art** TIME Magazine
Editor-in-Chief Sharon Coan, M.S.Ed.	**Interior Layout Designer** Robin Erickson

Publisher
Corinne Burton, M.A.Ed.

Shell Education
5301 Oceanus Drive
Huntington Beach, CA 92649-1030
http://www.shelleducation.com
ISBN 978-1-4258-0471-8

© 2008 Shell Education

Research on Using Biographies in Your Classroom

Narrative has long been an essential component of social studies education. How can you study colonization without helping students understand the struggles of the Jamestown settlement? How can you tell the story of the Civil War without exploring Abraham Lincoln? However, the distinction between these two cases provides a nutshell look at the way in which the classroom use of narrative is changing: the description of Jamestown is an institutional narrative—the story of a group, civilization, or entity; the description of Lincoln is the story of a person—a personal narrative or biography that we use as a window into the greater world.

It is likely that your textbook focuses on institutional narratives. Just look at the table of contents. Does it include chapters such as *From Empire to Independence, The Creation of the United States, The United States of North America, An Agrarian Republic,* and *The Growth of Democracy*? Certainly these chapters include narratives—the stories of cities, governments, and nations—and these narratives have the advantage of offering context for world events. However, the use of institutional narratives alone can leave many students disconnected from the material. Students may be unfamiliar with the ways institutions act. They have no framework for judging, for example, the actions of South Africa during Apartheid or the people of China during the cultural revolution. But students know how people act, and the study of personalities via biographies allows students to understand world events within the context of human motives and interactions (Donaldson 1986).

The study of personal narratives also encourages students to place themselves within the framework of history, helping them see that just as the people profiled in this book helped shape history, they also have the potential to influence the world around them. As Keith Barton and Linda Levstik (2004) write, "If the study of history never makes it to the personal level, students might come to regard humans as little more than pawns in a cosmic game of chess. For them to take responsibility for the common good, they must believe they have a role to play in creating the future." Certainly institutions create change, but by helping students see the individuals behind the institutions, you can help students understand their own active role in creating tomorrow's world.

And the use of individual narrative (e.g., biography) in the classroom is more than a sideshow technique used by maverick educators. In fact, the use of individual narrative as part of a balanced social studies curriculum was mandated by the reports of both the Bradley Commission (Jackson 1989) and the National Commission on Social Studies in the Schools (Mullins 1990), the latter of which also wrote, "The first priority [of a social studies curriculum] is in-depth study of selected topics to replace mere 'coverage' of content." This is a goal that is specifically commensurate with the in-depth study required by biography.

Primary Sources in This Book

TIME Magazine Covers as Primary Sources

The design of this book follows the recommendation from the National Commission on Social Studies in the Schools (NCSS): "that a rich variety of materials should be included in teaching and learning such as original sources . . . artifacts, photographs . . ." and that "the curriculum should balance study of the United States with studies of other cultures" (Mullins 1990). Integral to this book is the use of primary source material. Helping students explore authentic documents (e.g., TIME Magazine covers) allows students to form their own opinions about historical people and world events, rather than depending on an explanation filtered through a historian. This is similar to reading a poem rather than an explanation of what makes poetry or looking at a painting rather than reading an art review. Primary source activities are more engaging than traditional text and encourage students to ask questions. Primary sources allow students to use their creativity and their minds to formulate questions and find answers, rather than simply reading given answers in a textbook.

Quick Strategies to Use with TIME Covers

- Present contextual information after exploring the document itself. This allows students to form their own opinions, make predictions, and then use background information to fill in the gaps.

- Have students use magnifying glasses to study the cover in detail. What is in the background? What does the format of the document tell us about the society's technology? What does clothing, posture, title, prices, etc., tell us about societal norms?

- Let students use caption bubbles to enable the TIME person to speak to the class. What would this person say if he or she could speak to the class?

- After viewing a cover, have students generate a list of questions for an interview with this person. Then have students write the answers of what they think this person would say.

- When presenting background information, make sure to explore the origin of the document—Who created it? What was its purpose? What historical context made the document important?

- Divide the cover into quadrants and have four groups in the class analyze a different quadrant for what they see.

- Fold the cover in half vertically and let students create Venn diagrams to compare one side with the other side.

Primary Sources in This Book *(cont.)*

Quotations as Primary Sources

There are two "levels" of quotations in this book: direct quotations from historical figures and quotations from the biographies written to describe these people. The direct quotations, of course, are primary sources, which you can explore as such with your students. (Don't forget context!) But even the quotations written to describe these people are primary sources written by an author at the time the subject appeared in TIME Magazine. Entire lessons can center around these quotations. Consider the activities below when planning your lessons.

Quick Strategies to Use with Quotations

- Display thought-provoking phrases on a SMART Board™, digital projection system, or classroom chalkboard.

- Offer short quotation activities for completion by speedy finishers (extra credit or homework).

- Ask students to define what a quotation means to them.

- Have students rewrite a quotation in their own words.

- Challenge students to write two possible interpretations of the quotation.

- Let students respond to a quotation with an illustration or short answer.

- Give each student a different quotation. Have them walk around the room and say this quotation to as many different people as they can within a two-minute period of time.

Texts as Primary Sources

Today the impossibility of writing unbiased history is generally accepted. Even when looking through the long lens of history, with the best intentions, the choices historians make about inclusion of material forces viewpoints into the text. While primary sources are certainly not free of bias (in fact, the many forms of political propaganda are *very* biased), they allow students to make up their own minds about historical "right" and "wrong." They can provide the starting point for valuable discussion of historical bias. On the other hand, most texts leave little room for interpretation, and any included bias is generally presented as fact.

Quick Strategies to Use with Text

- Take an excerpt of the text and have students analyze it and write opinions about it.

- Have students use the text to highlight any words they do not know. These words can be used on spelling and vocabulary quizzes.

- Challenge students to find bias in the article. Then have them rewrite the article to make it less biased.

- If given the chance to interview this person, what questions would they ask? How do they think the person would answer these questions? Write the interview questions and the answers.

- After students read each paragraph, have them write down any remaining questions they have about the person.

Multiple Intelligences Overview

The Eight Multiple Intelligences

- The **Verbal/Linguistic** child thinks in words. He likes to write, read, play word games, and tell interesting stories. He needs diaries, books, and writing materials.

- The **Visual/Spatial** child thinks in pictures. He likes to draw, design, and doodle. He needs art supplies, building materials, video equipment, and puzzles.

- The **Rhythmic/Musical** child thinks in melodies and rhythms. He likes listening to music, making his own music, tapping to the rhythm, and singing. He needs to play musical instruments, see concerts, and use a karaoke machine.

- The **Intrapersonal** child keeps his thoughts to himself. He likes to set goals, meditate, and daydream. And, he enjoys quiet places. He needs time alone and prefers individualized projects.`

- The **Logical/Mathematical** child thinks by reasoning. She likes figuring out problems, puzzles, experimenting, and calculating. She needs science supplies, trips to museums, and math manipulatives.

- The **Bodily/Kinesthetic** child thinks by using her body. She likes dancing, moving, jumping, running, and touching. She needs movement, sports, theater, physical games, and hands-on activities.

- The **Interpersonal** child thinks by talking about her ideas to others. She likes organizing events, being the leader, partying, and mediating between friends. She needs time with friends, group projects, and social events.

- The **Naturalistic** child thinks by classifying. She likes studying anything in nature including rocks, animals, plants, and the weather. She needs time outside, nature hikes, telescopes, binoculars, and notebooks for classification.

Multiple Intelligences Overview *(cont.)*

Multiple Intelligences Focus for Each Lesson

Lesson	Multiple Intelligences
Compare and Contrast	logical/mathematical, verbal/linguistic, interpersonal
Defining Greatness	interpersonal, verbal/linguistic
Jigsaw Puzzle	visual/spatial, interpersonal, logical/mathematical
Autobiography	intrapersonal, verbal/linguistic
Biography Mural	intrapersonal, visual/spatial, bodily/kinesthetic
Poetry and Songs	interpersonal, rhythmic/musical, verbal/linguistic
Board Game	interpersonal, visual/spatial, logical/mathematical
Animal Comparison	intrapersonal, bodily/kinesthetic, naturalistic
Fact Sort	logical/mathematical, interpersonal, visual/spatial
Make TIME	intrapersonal, verbal/linguistic, bodily/kinesthetic
Choose Your Own Adventure	interpersonal, verbal/linguistic, logical/mathematical
Talking Hands	interpersonal, bodily/kinesthetic
A Complete Person	interpersonal, verbal/linguistic
Time Line Game	interpersonal, logical/mathematical, verbal/linguistic
Change the World	intrapersonal, bodily/kinesthetic, verbal/linguistic
TIME Cover	interpersonal, verbal/linguistic, logical/mathematical
Fun Facts Game	interpersonal, verbal/lingustic
Math Word Problems	logical/mathematical, interpersonal, verbal/lingustic
Skits	interpersonal, bodily/kinesthetic, verbal/lingustic
Biography Role-Play	intrapersonal, bodily/kinesthetic, linguistic

How To Use This Book

This collaboration with TIME Magazine is divided into two parts. The first part includes 20 ready-to-use biography strategy lessons that can apply to any person in history. To make it teacher friendly and easy to implement, the lessons refer to the biographies in the second part of the book. The second part includes TIME biographies about 60 diverse people who have shaped our world ethnically, culturally, geographically, and vocationally. Most of the people in this book are heroic, such as Martin Luther King Jr., Mother Teresa, and Mohandas Gandhi, but we have also included as educational counterpoint some of history's most controversial figures (Mao Zedong, Adolf Hitler, Joseph Stalin, and so on).

Each of the 60 people has a biography written in the format of an entertaining, interesting nonfiction article. With each biography is the actual TIME Magazine cover of the person profiled—use these valuable primary source documents to help students put faces to their studies. Each TIME cover is also included on the CD that accompanies this book, allowing you to display these covers at greater than life size and in full color, using a classroom projection system. Each biography also has a list of key dates in the person's life. Finally, strong comprehension and discussion questions are included to help your students further interact with the TIME covers and texts.

Many of these standards-based lessons are collaborative. Almost all of the 20 lessons incorporate active learning, and some are formatted as games. Use them to motivate your students and to enrich your existing social studies curriculum. This book also supports Howard Gardner's eight multiple intelligences, with lessons for every learning type.

If you have favorite biography lessons of your own, consider using the TIME covers and written biographies to augment your lessons. Here in compact and student-friendly format is a wealth of basic research materials, appropriate for use with any activity.

How This Book Is Differentiated

One way to differentiate curriculum is by using the model of multiple intelligences. In today's classrooms, there are a variety of learning styles, talents, and preferences. The multiple-intelligence model nurtures the broad range of talents in students. It identifies and categorizes eight different intelligences. Each lesson in this book is built around several different multiple intelligences, thus enabling teachers to meet students' needs.

How To Use This Book *(cont.)*

Summary of Biography Strategy Lessons

Compare and Contrast	Students will research historical figures and will then work in pairs or groups of three to make graphic organizer posters that compare and contrast these people.
Defining Greatness	After previewing several biographies, students will work in teams of 4–5 students to brainstorm creative words that describe these people. Teams will compete to brainstorm words that other teams did not list. Finally, teams will write definitions of these words and present them to the class.
Jigsaw Puzzle	Students will work in groups to put together jigsaw puzzles of TIME covers. After quickly exploring prior knowledge about the people on these covers, groups will use the biographies to write facts on the back of the jigsaw puzzle pieces.
Autobiography	Students will learn about the elements of a biography and will then use this format to write their own autobiographies.
Biography Mural	Students will explore several biographies and each student will then choose one person to present in an illustrated mural, showing scenes from this person's life.
Poetry and Songs	Students will explore several biographies and will then work in small groups to write and perform songs or poetry about their favorites.
Board Game	Students will research selected biographies focusing on the challenges faced by the subjects of the biographies as they worked toward their goals. Working in small groups, students will then use this information to create board games highlighting these challenges.
Animal Comparison	After working as a class to brainstorm the personality attributes of selected individuals, each student will make a poster comparing one of these people to an animal with similar attributes. This is one of the more basic lessons in this book.
Fact Sort	Groups will read the biographies of selected individuals, listing on the board as many facts as possible for each. Then, in a following class period, groups will compete to match facts with the correct person.
Make TIME	Students will explore the format of a biography and will then write and illustrate biographies of people they consider heroes for inclusion in a classroom version of TIME Magazine. This is one of the more involved and time-consuming lessons included in this book.
Choose Your Own Adventure	In this relatively advanced lesson, students will explore selected biographies before writing choose-your-own-adventure stories based on these people. What could these people's lives—and the world—have been like if they had made alternate decisions?

How To Use This Book *(cont.)*

Summary of Biography Strategy Lessons *(cont.)*

Talking Hands	Students will research and present information about selected biographies. Next, small groups will make posters of these people and will label posters with information about what these people did (hands), felt (heart), said (mouth), and experienced (eyes).
A Complete Person	After exploring biographies, pairs of students will each research an aspect of the lives of one of these individuals (background, key dates, achievements, death, fun fact). Students will then collaborate to organize and present all the information about their subjects. This lesson requires that students research their subjects.
Time Line Game	In this fun game, after exploring the selected biographies, groups will create lists of important events in the lives of these three people. Students will then trade lists with other groups and will have to use the knowledge they remember from the initial exploration to put the important events in order. The winning group earns a reward of your choice.
Change the World	After reading selected biographies, each student will choose one of the people as the subject for a poster showing what the world was like before this person was born and what it is like now (highlighting how each individual changed the world).
TIME Cover	Students will use the techniques of primary source document exploration to search for information in TIME covers and will then create their own magazine covers, hiding as many information clues as possible.
Fun Facts Game	Each student will research one fun fact about a selected individual. After making a list of these facts and then cutting them into slips, students will play a version of the game Balderdash® in which they compete to guess true facts while making up untrue ones to trick their classmates.
Math Word Problems	After exploring the selected biographies, students will work in pairs to write math word problems about these people. Groups can choose to present their word problems to the class, preferably in the math portion of the day.
Skits	Students will work in groups to write and present skits based on the lives of several individuals.
Biography Role-Play	Each student will "become" a famous individual from history and will answer prearranged questions. Depending on the time allocated to this activity, students can ask one another questions; or another class, parents, or community can interact with your in-character students.

Correlation to Standards

The No Child Left Behind (NCLB) legislation mandates that all states adopt academic standards that identify the skills students will learn in kindergarten through grade 12. While many states had already adopted academic standards prior to NCLB, the legislation set requirements to ensure the standards were detailed and comprehensive.

Standards are designed to focus instruction and guide adoption of curricula. Standards are statements that describe the criteria necessary for students to meet specific academic goals. They define the knowledge, skills, and content students should acquire at each level. Standards are also used to develop standardized tests to evaluate students' academic progress.

In many states today, teachers are required to demonstrate how their lessons meet state standards. State standards are used in the development of Shell Education products, so educators can be assured that they meet the academic requirements of each state.

How to Find Your State Correlations

Shell Education is committed to producing educational materials that are research and standards based. In this effort, all products are correlated to the academic standards of the 50 states, the District of Columbia, and the Department of Defense Dependent Schools. A correlation report customized for your state can be printed directly from the following website:
http://www.shelleducation.com.

If you require assistance in printing correlation reports, please contact Customer Service at 1-877-777-3450.

McREL Compendium

Shell Education uses the Mid-continent Research for Education and Learning (McREL) Compendium to create standards correlations. Each year, McREL analyzes state standards and revises the compendium. By following this procedure, they are able to produce a general compilation of national standards.

Each reading-comprehension strategy assessed in this book is based on one or more McREL content standards. The chart on the next two pages shows the McREL standards that correlate to each lesson used in the book. To see a state-specific correlation, visit the Shell Education website at **http://www.shelleducation.com.**

Correlation to Standards *(cont.)*

McREL Compendium *(cont.)*

Lesson	Standard 1	Standard 2
Compare and Contrast	Students will summarize and paraphrase information in texts.	Students will use prewriting strategies to plan written work (e.g., uses graphic organizers, groups related ideas).
Defining Greatness	Students will use descriptive language that clarifies and enhances ideas.	Students will use word reference materials to determine the meaning of unknown words.
Jigsaw Puzzle	Students will summarize and paraphrase information in texts.	Students will use reading skills and strategies to understand a variety of informational texts.
Autobiography	Students will write autobiographical compositions (e.g. uses simple narrative strategies and provides some insight into why this incident is memorable).	Students will use the general skills and strategies of the writing process.
Biography Mural	Students will use strategies to edit and publish written work (e.g., selects presentation format according to purpose, incorporates illustrations).	Students will establish a purpose for reading (e.g., for information, to understand a specific viewpoint).
Poetry and Songs	Students will write narrative accounts, such as poems (e.g., develops characters, creates an organizing structure, sequences events, uses an identifiable voice).	Students will use a variety of sentence structures in writing (e.g., expands basic sentence patterns).
Board Game	Students will summarize and paraphrase information in texts.	Students will use prewriting strategies to plan written work (e.g., brainstorms ideas, organizes information according to type and purpose of writing).
Animal Comparison	Students will contribute to group discussions.	Students will use prewriting strategies to plan written work (e.g., brainstorms).
Fact Sort	Students will summarize and paraphrase information in texts (e.g., includes the main idea and significant supporting details of a reading selection).	Students will write expository compositions (e.g., develops the topic with simple facts, excludes extraneous information).
Make TIME	Students will use the general skills and strategies of the writing process.	Students will understand structural patterns or organization in informational texts (e.g., chronological, logical or sequential order).

Correlation to Standards *(cont.)*

McREL Compendium *(cont.)*

Lesson	Standard 1	Standard 2
Choose Your Own Adventure	Students will use the general skills and strategies of the writing process.	Students will contribute to group discussions.
Talking Hands	Students will use strategies to edit and publish written work (e.g., selects presentation format according to purpose, incorporates illustrations).	Students will organize ideas for oral presentation (e.g., uses notes or other memory aids, organizes ideas around major points).
A Complete Person	Students will use a variety of strategies to plan research (e.g., organizes prior knowledge about a topic, develops a course of action, determines how to locate necessary information).	Students will make basic oral presentations to the class (e.g., includes content appropriate to the audience, incorporates several sources of information).
Time Line Game	Students will summarize and paraphrase information in texts.	Students will use prewriting strategies to plan written work (e.g., brainstorms).
Change the World	Students will use strategies to edit and publish written work (e.g. incorporates information, shares finished product).	Students will summarize and paraphrase information in texts.
TIME Cover	Students will understand the use and meaning of symbols and images in visual media (e.g., the dependence of symbols on shared social and cultural understandings).	Students will use the general skills and strategies of the writing process.
Fun Facts Game	Students will use a variety of strategies to plan research (e.g. develops a course of action, determines how to locate necessary information).	Students will make basic oral presentations to the class (e.g., uses subject-related information and vocabulary).
Math Word Problems	Students will use strategies (e.g., adapts organization, form) to write for a variety of purposes.	Students will organize ideas for oral presentations (e.g., uses notes or other memory aids).
Skits	Students will make basic oral presentations to the class (e.g., relates ideas and observations, incorporates visual aids or props, incorporates several sources of information).	Students will use prewriting strategies to plan written work (e.g., uses graphic organizers, groups related ideas).
Biography Role-Play	Students will organize ideas for oral presentations (e.g., uses notes or other memory aids, organizes ideas around major points, uses traditional structures such as posing and answering a question).	Students will write in response to literature (e.g., summarizes main ideas and significant details).

Biography Strategy Lessons

Compare and Contrast

Lesson Summary

Students will research historical figures and will then work in pairs or groups of three to make graphic organizer posters that compare and contrast these people. You may either choose the biographies for your students (easier) or apply this lesson to historical figures of students' choice (more advanced).

Objectives

- Students will summarize and paraphrase information in texts.
- Students will use prewriting strategies to plan written work (e.g., uses graphic organizers, groups related ideas).

Multiple Intelligences

- verbal/linguistic
- logical/mathematical
- interpersonal

Materials

- notebook paper
- large paper or poster boards
- pens, crayons, markers

Preparation

1. Copy a different TIME biography for each of your students.

2. Make a class list to use with the assessment.

3. Copy the rubric in the assessment section to grade students' presentations.

Procedure

1. Ask students to help you brainstorm famous people. Have the class choose one famous person who most students know well. (In this step, it is okay if students pick an athlete or music star.) Write this person's name on your classroom board.

2. Ask students to imagine you (the teacher) have never heard of this person. (This may be true!) How would they describe this person to you? Who is he or she? What is he or she famous for? What ethnicity? What gender? What has he or she done to help others? Write this information on your board and leave it there for later use. Note: If you like, list this information in the format of a mind map (bubble web) and explore this method of organizing information.

3. Explain that each student will be researching an historical figure and writing biographical information about this person, similar to what the class just did.

4. Preview the TIME covers of your choosing. (Each image is on the CD if you want to show them to the class using a projection system.)

Compare and Contrast *(cont.)*

Procedure *(cont.)*

5. Give each student one copy of a TIME cover with background information. Ask them to read this information and, on their own paper, write 10 facts they learned. Support students as needed during this independent work time.

6. Quickly check that all students have written 10 facts about their historical figures. (This may be the end of the class period.) Make sure that students keep these sheets for later use, or have students turn them in to you so that these sheets are not lost.

7. Explain how to use a Venn diagram to compare and contrast information:

   - Revisit the famous person you used as an example at the beginning of this lesson.

   - Brainstorm and add information for another famous person.

   - Draw a two-circle Venn diagram on your classroom board.

   - Write information unique to person #1 in the left side of the diagram.

   - Then, write information unique to person #2 in the right portion of the diagram.

   - Finally, write information common to both people in the area where the circles overlap.

8. Explain that students will now be working in pairs to make Venn diagram posters that compare and contrast their historical figures, just as you did on the classroom board.

9. Have students work with partners. Make sure that each student in each pair has a different biography.

10. Distribute poster supplies or indicate where students can find these supplies in the classroom. Explain any additional expectations (poster title, students' names on the back, illustrations, etc.).

11. Allow time for pairs to complete their Venn diagram posters. Support students as necessary.

12. Ask pairs to present their Venn diagram posters to the class. They should answer these three questions at a minimum:

    - Who are the people they researched?

    - What is unique about each of them?

    - What do these two people share?

Compare and Contrast *(cont.)*

Differentiation Strategies

- **Above grade level**—Have these students work in threes instead of pairs, using the three-ring version of the Venn diagram.

- **Below grade level**—For students who need more support, reduce the number of facts each student needs to find. Instead of 10, have students find five facts. Or, you can define the facts they need to find when reading about their historical figures. For example, when was this person alive? Is he or she American or not? What did he or she do?

- **English language learners**—Have parent volunteers work with these students in small groups. If that is not possible, extend the time needed for this activity. Allow one class period for the introduction and full-class brainstorming activity, one class period for individual research, one class period working in pairs/threes to make posters, and half a class period to present these posters.

Assessment

1. Use over-the-shoulder assessment as you walk around the classroom, checking off students' names or offering a quick score from 1–10 as they finish writing their 10 facts.

2. Assess students' Venn diagram presentations using the following rubric.

All categories are worth 10 points for a total of 30 points.

Preparation	The student had all necessary materials.
Delivery	The student made eye contact, spoke loud enough, and presented his or her information clearly.
Effort	The student did his or her best, had accurate information, and the overall presentation was a success.

Defining Greatness

Lesson Summary

After previewing several biographies, students will work in teams of 4–5 students to brainstorm creative words that describe these people. Teams will compete to brainstorm words that other teams did not list. Finally, teams will write definitions of these words and present them to the class.

Objectives

- Students will use descriptive language that clarifies and enhances ideas.
- Students will use word reference materials to determine the meaning of unknown words.

Multiple Intelligences

- verbal/linguistic
- interpersonal

Materials

- notebook paper
- pens and pencils

Preparation

1. Choose two or three TIME biographies and copy them for your students. (Students will be in small groups and each group will need a copy of all the biographies for this lesson.)

2. Make a class list to use with the assessment.

3. Copy the *Traits of Good Writing* in the assessment section to grade students' work.

Procedure

1. Preview the selected biographies using the following technique:

   - Display one TIME cover. (Each image is on the CD if you want to show them to the class using a projection system.)

   - Ask students what they know about this person.

   - What clues does the TIME cover offer to help students extend this background knowledge? What can they discover from this document? (Look at clothing, text, symbols, etc.)

2. Use popcorn reading or the class reading strategy of your choice to read aloud the accompanying biography. (For popcorn reading, chose one student to begin. After reading a paragraph, he or she will say "Popcorn to . . ." and then another student's name.)

   - Ask students what they learned about this person.

   - Repeat with this lesson's other remaining people.

Defining Greatness *(cont.)*

Procedure *(cont.)*

3. Ask the class to brainstorm a few words that relate to these people. For example, what does the word *pioneer* mean (Orville Wright)? Or, what is an *inauguration* (George Bush)? Do not brainstorm too many words! This step is only an example of the procedure you will be asking students to do independently.

4. Explain that students will be working in teams (groups of 4–5 work well) to brainstorm words that relate to these people, using the procedure you just previewed as a class. Split students into groups and assign each group a number.

5. Tell groups they are now competing to brainstorm words that no other group lists—for each unique word, they will earn a point. The winning team will earn a small classroom reward of your choice. Make sure each group chooses a student to take notes, and then distribute copies of the biographies (each team gets all the biographies). Allow an appropriate amount of time (15 minutes) for each team to create a list of words for each person.

6. Reconvene as a class. Ask the first group to read aloud the words from its list. As the list is being read, if another group has the same word, have both (or all) groups cross this word off their list. List the first group's unique words on your classroom board.

7. Continue this procedure with each group, listing each team's unique words on the classroom board. Make sure words relate to the biographies and ask groups to explain any nebulous connections. At the end, the team with the most unique words wins.

8. Explain that students will now be working individually to write definitions for these unique words. Divide the words among your class such that each student has an appropriate number of words (2–5 words, depending on the length of the initial list and on available time).

9. Preview dictionaries or online resources that students can use to look up definitions.

10. Allow an appropriate amount of time for students to look up their words and write definitions. Encourage students to use their own words, rather than copying definitions directly. Model how to do this with an example on the board.

11. Either have students turn in their definitions to you or ask them to present definitions to the class.

Defining Greatness *(cont.)*

Differentiation Strategies

- **Above grade level**—As you play the vocabulary game, offer teams an additional half point if they can use context clues within the written biography to define their words instead of using a dictionary. If the team can't define a word, another team can steal this half point by offering a correct definition. At the end of the game, this will leave you with a depleted vocabulary list, perhaps requiring you to abbreviate the last part of the lesson.

- **Below grade level**—Instead of working independently in Steps 8–11, support struggling students by asking them to work in pairs.

- **English language learners**—Assign each team only one biography. Instead of the described vocabulary game, have teams scan their biographies for 3–5 words they don't know. Have teams work together to write definitions of these words.

Assessment

1. Use over-the-shoulder assessment and your class list to assign students a quick score from 1–10 while they are working in groups to brainstorm words. (You can base this on involvement and effort as well as on results.)

2. Have students turn in their written definitions and use the *Traits of Good Writing* or the assessment strategy with which you are most comfortable. *Traits of Good Writing* include:

   - Ideas that are interesting and important
   - Ideas are the heart of the piece
   - Organization that is logical and effective
   - Voice that is individual and appropriate
   - Word choice that is specific and memorable
   - Sentence fluency that is smooth and expressive
   - Conventions that are correct and communicative

Jigsaw Puzzle

Lesson Summary

Students will work in groups to put together jigsaw puzzles of TIME covers. After quickly exploring prior knowledge about the people on these covers, groups will use the biographies to write facts on the back of the jigsaw puzzle pieces.

Objectives

- Students will summarize and paraphrase information in texts.
- Students will use reading skills and strategies to understand a variety of informational texts.

Multiple Intelligences

- visual/spatial
- interpersonal
- logical/mathematical

Materials

- notebook paper and writing utensils
- clear tape (each team will need a roll)
- small plastic bags (to keep jigsaw pieces organized)

Preparation

1. Choose various TIME biographies and copy them for your students. (Each small group of students will need one TIME cover and the corresponding written biography. Each group should have a different biography.)

2. For each team, cut one TIME cover into jigsaw puzzle pieces. Depending on your class level, 5–10 pieces works well. Organize these pieces in plastic bags.

3. Make a class list to use with the assessment.

4. Copy the rubric in the assessment section to grade students' work.

Procedure

1. Split students into groups (2–5 students works well). Smaller groups work well with a more advanced class.

2. Distribute a jigsaw puzzle bag to each group and explain that the groups will be racing to complete their puzzles. On your signal, allow groups to open their puzzle bags, and allow an appropriate amount of time for students to complete their puzzles, laying the pieces on a desk. (Don't tape them yet!)

3. Once groups have completed their puzzles, explore this lesson's people. Do students recognize them? If so, who are they? If not, do they have any guesses as to what these people might have done? When do they think these people lived? Use the clues of the TIME covers to explore the individuals.

Jigsaw Puzzle *(cont.)*

Procedure *(cont.)*

4. Give each group the written biography that matches its puzzle.

5. Have each group use the biographies to write facts about the people on the back of jigsaw puzzle pieces. There should only be one fact per puzzle piece. These facts should be different from those already covered as a class. Encourage students to find interesting, unusual, or creative facts.

6. Explain that groups will now be switching puzzles using the following procedure:

   - On designated table space, each group will place its puzzle pieces face down, fact up, with the pieces disorganized.

   - On your signal, groups will rotate so they are in front of another group's puzzle.

   - Groups may not turn over the pieces! Instead, they will put the pieces together fact-side up, taping them together when they are finished.

   - When groups have taped their puzzle pieces together, they should use the facts to guess which person is on the other side.

   - On your signal, groups may turn over their puzzles to see if their guesses are correct.

7. Reconvene as a class to debrief the lesson, exploring the interesting facts students learned, both while reading the biographies and from the backs of other groups' puzzle pieces.

Jigsaw Puzzle *(cont.)*

Differentiation Strategies

- **Above grade level**—Cut TIME covers into small jigsaw puzzle pieces. Also, have students work in pairs instead of larger teams.

- **Below grade level**—Create larger teams, supporting struggling students with motivated teammates.

- **English language learners**—First, give a few examples for students to write on the backs of their puzzle pieces. Then, offer suggestions for the other facts students need to find. (For example, *when did this person live? What did he or she do? How did this person help others? What is one thing you find interesting?*

Assessment

1. Use the questions listed below to assess your students. Write them on the board and have each student answer them on a separate sheet of paper. Tell students that they will be assessed on their answers and how they performed in their groups.

   - I contributed at least two facts to my group.
     (yes or no)

   - The facts I contributed to my group are:

   - What I wrote is accurate.
     (yes or no)

   - I helped other group members find facts.
     (yes or no)

2. Collect completed puzzles and assess the facts using an assessment strategy of your choice. (Make sure students put all group members' names on the puzzle!)

Autobiography

Lesson Summary

Students will learn the elements of a biography and will then use this format to write their own autobiographies.

Objectives

- Students will write autobiographical compositions (e.g., uses simple narrative strategies and provides some insight into why this incident is memorable).
- Students will use the general skills and strategies of the writing process.

Multiple Intelligences

- verbal/linguistic
- intrapersonal

Materials

- notebook paper and writing utensils

Preparation

1. Choose a few different TIME biographies and copy them for your students. (Each group of three students will need one of these biographies.)

2. Make a class list to use with the assessment.

3. Copy the *6+1 Trait Writing* in the assessment section to grade students' work.

Procedure

1. One at a time, display the selected TIME covers. (Each image is on the CD if you want to show them to the class using a projection system.) Briefly discuss students' prior knowledge of these people: What do they know and what questions do they have at this point? What questions do students expect would be answered in written biographies of these people?

2. Split students into groups of three and give each group a copy of one of the TIME biographies.

3. Each group will now write several questions that are answered in the biography, such as *When was this person born?* Allow appropriate time for completion and support struggling groups, as necessary.

4. Reconvene the class and have each group present the questions answered by the biography it explored. List these questions on your classroom board. (You do not need to keep a separate list for each person—one master list of questions is fine.)

Autobiography *(cont.)*

Procedure *(cont.)*

5. Once you have a list of questions, ask students if there are any more important questions they think should be added to this list—what important questions do biographies answer?

6. With students' help, decide on the top four important questions that a biography needs to answer. Circle these questions on your classroom board.

7. Explain that students will now be writing autobiographies—each autobiography needs to answer the questions you just circled.

8. Define your expectations for the biography assignment. Depending on your class level and the amount of time you allocate to this activity, choose one of the following formats:

   • A paragraph-format writing assignment, using each step of the writing process. In this case, ask students to answer the biography questions you chose as a class, and then have students use these answers as the prewriting stage of the writing process. This can be a useful beginning-of-the-year activity, especially if you encourage peer group revisions later in the writing process, as students can use this time to get to know their classmates.

   • An abbreviated paragraph-format writing assignment. Have students answer the questions you chose as a class in paragraph format, but do not explicitly follow the steps of the writing process. Ask students to write short answers to the questions and turn these answers in to you.

9. Allow appropriate time for completion.

10. If you like, have students present their autobiographies to the class. When finished, collect the assignments.

Autobiography *(cont.)*

Differentiation Strategies

- **Above grade level**—Give each group all the selected TIME biographies (or have them rotate biographies, passing them to another group after a given period of time). Have groups read all the biographies and then ask that their lists of questions include only the questions common across all the biographies. (What questions do all of the biographies answer?)

- **Below grade level**—Instead of asking students to write autobiographies in paragraph form, have them write short answers to each agreed-upon autobiographical question. Also, reduce the overall number of questions.

- **English language learners**— Have students illustrate their autobiographical events in poster format, and then ask them to caption these illustrations, as appropriate.

Assessment

1. Use over-the-shoulder assessment while students are working in groups, assigning a score from 1–10 based on effort and involvement.

2. Collect (or display) completed autobiographies and use the *6 + 1 Trait Writing* to assign points as appropriate. The *6+1 Trait Writing* uses the following points to assess:

   - Ideas and content—Does the writing focus on the main idea?

   - Organization—Does it have a beginning, middle, and end?

   - Voice—Is there a real person behind the words?

   - Word choice—Does the writer use rich and powerful words?

   - Sentence fluency—Does the text flow smoothly?

   - Conventions—Are the spelling and grammar correct?

   - Presentation (if applicable)—Is the writing legible?

Biography Mural

Lesson Summary

Students will explore several biographies and each student will then choose one person to present in an illustrated mural, showing scenes from this person's life.

Objectives

- Students will use strategies to edit and publish written work (e.g., selects presentation format according to purpose, incorporates illustrations).

- Students will establish a purpose for reading (e.g., for information, to understand a specific viewpoint).

Multiple Intelligences

- visual/spatial
- intrapersonal
- bodily/kinesthetic

Materials

- notebook paper and writing utensils
- large paper or poster board
- pens, crayons, markers

Preparation

1. Choose a few TIME biographies to present to the class. (After this activity's first class period, each student will choose to focus on one of the biographies—make copies based on how many students choose each person.)

2. Make a class list to use with the assessment.

3. Copy the rubric in the assessment section to grade students' work.

Procedure

1. Preview each of this lesson's TIME biographies using the following procedure:

   - Display one person's TIME cover. (Each image is on the CD if you want to show them to the class using a projection system.)

   - Ask students what they know about the person on display. With many of these individuals, students will need to use the context clues of the TIME cover to make educated guesses about the person. Make this a game: students are investigators trying to guess the identity and accomplishments of these people.

   - Once students feel as if they have exhausted their investigation based on the TIME cover, offer a short description of each of these individuals. (Don't yet read aloud the accompanying written biography.) Were students' guesses correct?

   - Work as a class to create one-sentence descriptions of these people.

Biography Mural *(cont.)*

Procedure *(cont.)*

2. Explain that each student will now choose one of these people on which to focus. Ask students to think (but do not say aloud) which person they would like to explore in depth.

3. To avoid your entire class choosing the same person, have students put their heads down on their desks and close their eyes. Say the subjects' names one at a time and have students raise their hands when they hear the name they want. On your class list, mark the initials of the selected person next to each student's name. Time this to be the end of a class period (or have enough copies of the written biographies on hand so that each student can have a copy of the person they choose).

4. Explain that each student will now be making a poster of his or her person. This poster will show 4–8 scenes from this person's life. Preview any additional poster directions you think necessary (name on the back, colorful title, formatting specifics, etc.).

5. Distribute the appropriate written biographies and point students to the area in the room where they can find poster supplies. Allow appropriate time for students to read biographies and create their posters. Offer help as needed.

6. If time permits, have each student present his or her poster to the class, explaining why he or she chose these specific scenes.

Biography Mural *(cont.)*

Differentiation Strategies

- **Above grade level**—Increase the number of scenes each poster must include. When students present their posters, ask them to explain the posters as if they were narrating this person's life (in chronological order, using the pictures as visual representations of the major events in the person's life).

- **Below grade level**—Have students work with partners to make posters. Enlist the help of parent volunteers to aid these students as they work on their projects.

- **English language learners**—Group these students together and explore the written biographies orally (instead of asking students to read photocopied biographies on their own). One successful strategy for reading these aloud is to split the group into three smaller groups. Then, each group can then present on one biography together.

Assessment

1. Have students present their finished biography posters and use the assessment rubric below to assign an appropriate number of points.

2. Score students 1–10 based on the following:

   - Organization—Was it easy to read? Did it communicate the information?

   - Content—Is it accurate? Were the main facts covered?

   - Creativity—Was the poster design interesting? What made it unique?

   - Speaking skills—Did he or she make eye contact? Could the class hear him or her? Did he or she cover the necessary material?

Poetry and Songs

Preparation

1. Choose three different TIME biographies and copy them for your students. (There will be three groups in the class. Each group will need a different TIME biography.)

2. Make a class list to use with the assessment.

3. Copy both of the assessment rubrics in the assessment section.

Procedure

1. Explain that you will be splitting the class into three groups and that each group will be presenting a different biography. Each group will read its biography and list enough facts so that during its presentation, each student in the group will have at least one thing to offer. If you like, designate one person in each group as leader and ask another student in each group to take notes.

2. Divide your class into three groups and give each group a different TIME biography (cover, biography, and time line).

3. Write the assessment rubric on the board before students begin so that students can see how they will be graded.

4. Allow appropriate time for groups to explore their biographies and to write facts. Toward the end of this time, encourage groups to organize and practice their presentations. One student should introduce the group's subject and then the remaining students should present, in an orderly fashion, the facts the group discovered. Encourage students to add creativity to their information and presentations. These presentations will be graded by their peers.

Poetry and Songs *(cont.)*

Procedure *(cont.)*

5. As groups present, display the relevant TIME cover. (Each image is on the CD if you want to show them to the class using a projection system.)

6. After each group presents, ask the audience to answer questions about the biography. *Who is this person? What are his or her major achievements? Would they want to be this person? Why or why not?*

7. Explain that students will be working in smaller groups to write songs or poetry about these individuals. To avoid having all students pick the same person, write the biography names on small pieces of paper and then place them in a bag, hat, or bucket. Let students take turns drawing one piece out of the bag. The name that each student draws will be the person for whom he or she writes the song or poem in this part of the activity. Group students together based on the individuals they chose.

8. Offer the following directions:

   • Each group will write and perform a song or a poem about its person.

   • Encourage students to keep in mind the facts they learned about these people, and define the number of facts each song must include (2–5 works well).

   • Depending on your class level, offer additional directions on how groups should go about creating songs/poems. This may include demonstrating this procedure as a class using a famous person most students know as an example. Also, define any additional format requirements, such as rhyme scheme, stanzas, etc.

9. Give each group a copy of its chosen biography. Allow appropriate time for groups to complete their songs/poems. As students finish their songs/poems, encourage students to practice presenting them just as you did with the initial, large-group presentations.

10. Have each small group perform its song/poem in front of the class. This can be intimidating, so be sure to set audience expectation guidelines beforehand, including respectful listening and applause at the end of each performance.

Poetry and Songs *(cont.)*

Differentiation Strategies

- **Above grade level**—Consider requiring these songs/poems to contain 4–6 facts. You can also ask that these songs/poems rhyme, or that they meet other style requirements (stanzas, limerick format, etc.).

- **Below grade level**—Instead of asking students to create full poems/songs, have them set facts to rhymes. Ask each small group of 2–3 students to pick one or two facts from the biography and then present these facts as rhymes.

- **English language learners**—Instead of asking your English language learners to present facts from this lesson's biographies, assist these students and explore these biographies as a group. For each, display the TIME cover and then use the classroom reading strategy of your choice to read aloud the accompanying biography. Then, spend additional time previewing and practicing song/poem format (and narrowly define the format you expect students to follow—a limerick works well). Scaffold students toward independence by demonstrating how to create a song/poem, creating one as a class and asking students to use the same procedure to create their own songs/poems.

Assessment

1. As groups present their biographies, let the class assess their peers. Copy the following rubric for students to judge the two other groups.

   1 = weak
   2 = average
   3 = strong

   - The presentation was easy to understand.
   - The presentation had important information.
   - Everyone in the group participated.
   - The presentation or information was creative.

2. After all students present their songs and poems, have each student write a self-assessment on his or her presentation. Tell students that the self-assessment will be averaged with the peer assessment. Copy the following rubric for students to judge their own work.

   1 = weak
   2 = average
   3 = strong

   - I contributed my ideas to the song or poem.
   - I stayed on the topic as my group worked.
   - I listened to others in my group when they were speaking.
   - During the presentation, I spoke/sang so that everyone could hear.

Board Game

Lesson Summary

Students will research selected biographies focusing on the challenges faced by the subjects of the biographies as they worked toward their goals. Working in small groups, students will then use this information to create board games highlighting these challenges.

Objectives

- Students will summarize and paraphrase information in texts.
- Students will use prewriting strategies to plan written work (e.g., brainstorms ideas, organizes information according to type and purpose of writing).

Multiple Intelligences

- visual/spatial
- interpersonal
- logical/mathematical

Materials

- notebook paper and writing utensils
- large paper, construction paper, cardboard
- pens, markers, crayons

Preparation

1. Choose three to five TIME biographies and copy all of them for your students.

2. Organize board game supplies. Bring in sample board games for students to see.

3. Make a class list to use with the assessment.

4. Make copies of the peer assessment in the assessment section.

Procedure

1. Ask students to help you brainstorm a definition for *hero*. Lead them to include in this definition the idea that every hero had to struggle through adversity to achieve his or her goals. Explore famous people that students know and ask them if they would—by this definition—consider these people heroes.

2. Show students copies of the TIME biographies and explore the lives of the subjects using the following procedure.
   - Display a TIME cover. (Each image is on the CD if you want to show them to the class using a projection system.)
   - Ask students what they already know about this person.
   - Use popcorn reading or the classroom reading strategy of your choice to read aloud the accompanying biography.
   - On your classroom board, write the person's name, and then under this write the headings *goals* and *challenges*.
   - Work with your class to brainstorm and list the person's goals and challenges. Leave these on the board for later use.
   - Repeat this procedure with this lesson's remaining people.

Board Game *(cont.)*

Procedure *(cont.)*

3. Ask students what they know about board games like Candyland®, Monopoly®, and Chutes and Ladders®. Lead them to realize that in each of these games there are goals and challenges. If possible, explore examples of each game. Ask students to offer additional examples of the goals and challenges of board games.

4. Explain that students will now be working in small groups to make board games based on the three to five people you explored earlier in the lesson. These board games will highlight goals and challenges (refer students to the lists on your classroom board). Ask your class to quickly brainstorm how they could represent a few of these challenges in board game format. How are board games organized? What are some common formats?

5. Either allow students to form their own small groups (3–4 students each) or divide students into groups of your choice.

6. Ask groups to brainstorm ideas for their board games. Each group needs to offer you a quick description of its game before starting construction. This cuts down on wasted supplies.

7. Once students have game approval, give them the board game supplies (large paper, pens, cardboard, crayons, etc.) and allow appropriate time for them to complete their board game designs (up to two full class periods).

8. When all groups have finished their board games, mix groups and allow time to play these games. It works well to have one member of the original group travel with the game in order to explain directions and help troubleshoot rules as problems arise.

9. Have groups turn in their games and display them in the classroom.

Board Game *(cont.)*

Differentiation Strategies

- **Above grade level**—Define a specific number of challenges that each board game must include. Ask groups to write the rules to their game and then, instead of explaining the games orally to the group that actually plays it, have this second group depend on the written rules. Encourage students to give one another feedback about their games. If time permits, allow groups to revise their games.

- **Below grade level**—On scratch paper, have groups illustrate plans for their board games before starting construction. This plan should show the general format (What will the board look like? How will pieces move?) as well as how the group plans to represent challenges and goals. If students have trouble with the planning phase, model this for them using graphic organizers.

- **English language learners**—After listing challenges and goals on your classroom board and splitting students into groups, have each group circle one challenge and one goal they will use in their board game. Ask each group to explain verbally how they will represent their challenge and goal before allowing them to start construction. Assist these students as necessary.

Assessment

1. While groups are working on their board games, circulate and offer each student a quick score from 1–10, based on effort and involvement.

2. Have students write peer evaluations after playing the games. Students can answer *yes* or *no* to the following three questions. If students answer no to any of the questions, they should write an explanation next to it.

   - The game rules are easy to understand.
   - The game taught me something new about the person.
   - The game design is creative and well organized.

Animal Comparison

Lesson Summary

After working as a class to brainstorm the personality attributes of selected individuals, each student will make a poster comparing one of these people to an animal with similar attributes. This is one of the more basic lessons in this book.

Objectives

- Students will contribute to group discussions.
- Students will use prewriting strategies to plan written work (e.g., brainstorms).

Multiple Intelligences

- intrapersonal
- bodily/kinesthetic
- naturalistic

Materials

- large paper or poster board
- pens, crayons, markers

Preparation

1. Organize poster supplies, making them easily accessible.

2. Copy the selected biographies you want to use for this lesson (3–5 biographies works well for this lesson).

3. Make copies of the assessment rubric to grade students' posters.

Procedure

1. Ask students how they think heroes are made—do people become heroes through their own actions, through historical circumstance, or is it a combination of both? Ask students if anyone can be a hero or if heroes are somehow different from everybody else. As examples, explore heroes that students know. Lead students to understand that heroes have to show certain character traits (courage, perseverance, motivation, intelligence, etc.), but that anyone can be a hero. Some heroes are famous, but many more heroes live among us without recognition.

2. Explain that in this lesson, they will be exploring three heroes. But instead of looking only at what these heroes *did*, they will be trying to figure out what personality traits allowed these people to become heroes.

Animal Comparison *(cont.)*

Procedure *(cont.)*

3. Explore each of this lesson's biographies using the following technique.

   - Display a person's TIME cover. (Each image is on the CD if you want to show them to the class using a projection system.)

   - Ask students what they already know about this person.

   - Have students read through the background information with partners using the paired reading strategy—students take turns reading paragraphs until they finish the information.

   - Write the person's name on your classroom board and ask your class to brainstorm the personality traits they associate with this person. Spend time on this step, searching for non-obvious traits (other than courage and persistence). Leave these traits on your board for later use.

   - Repeat this procedure with this lesson's remaining people.

4. Congratulate students on the lists they helped create. Pretend as if you need to erase the list—pick up an eraser and tell students they will need to memorize the list for use later in the lesson. Students will likely protest!

5. Explain that you were just kidding— you are not going to erase the list—but you will be teaching them a way to remember the items on this list using something called a *mnemonic*. A mnemonic is a trick that aids memory. In this case, each student will create a poster comparing one of these three people to an animal that shares the same attributes. If students can remember the animal, then this visual mnemonic will help them also remember the personality traits of the person the animal represents.

6. Give students five minutes to pick one of the TIME people and to think of an animal that has the same attributes as those listed beneath the person they chose. What animal is their person like?

7. Indicate where students can find poster supplies and define the amount of time they have to complete their posters. In addition to illustrating their person and the animal they chose to represent this person, each student should list the attributes the person and animal share. As students work, circulate through the room offering help and encouragement as needed.

8. Once students have finished, have them present their posters to the class. Ask each presenter to focus on why they chose this animal to represent this person—what personality traits do they share?

9. Collect finished posters and display them in your room.

Animal Comparison *(cont.)*

Differentiation Strategies

- **Above grade level**—Have each student divide his or her poster into sections and compare each of this lesson's people to an animal (instead of just picking one person and one animal). Also, have students write a sentence or two in each section that explains their choices.

- **Below grade level**—Group these students together and read the biography information aloud to them. To further simplify the lesson, take one person and model aloud how to brainstorm an animal that best matches each person.

- **English language learners**—Pair these students with two others who are proficient in the language for the biography reading. They can listen as their groups read aloud. Ask English language learners to contribute animals that are native to their region or country of origin.

Assessment

1. As students present their animal posters to the class, score them on their posters using the following rubric.

   1 = weak
   2 = average
   3 = strong

   - Grabs the audience's attention
   - Uses color and symbols
   - Contains information relevant to the individual
   - Is neat and readable
   - Follows directions
   - Shows creative skills

Fact Sort

Lesson Summary

Groups will read the biographies of selected individuals, listing on the board as many facts as possible for each. Then, in a following class period, groups will compete to match facts with the correct person.

Objectives

- Students will summarize and paraphrase information in texts (e.g., includes the main idea and significant supporting details of a reading selection).
- Students will write expository compositions (e.g., develops the topic with simple facts, excludes extraneous information).

Multiple Intelligences

- visual/spatial
- logical/mathematical
- interpersonal

Materials

- notebook paper and writing utensils
- clear tape (one roll per small group)
- small bags

Preparation

1. Copy the selected TIME biographies that you want to use for this lesson. (Each group of students will need a different TIME biography.)

2. Preparation is needed between the first and second days of this activity and is described in Step 5 of the Procedure section.

Procedure

1. Divide students into groups (3–4 students in each group works well) and explain that each group will be reading a different biography and making a list of as many facts as they can find.

2. Give each group one written biography and allow groups an appropriate amount of time to read the biography and list facts. Pair your English language learners and below-grade-level students with strong readers.

3. Reconvene as a class. Explore each of these three people using the following technique:

   - Write each of the people's names on your classroom board and display his or her TIME cover under his or her name. (Each image is on the CD if you want to show them to the class using a projection system.)

   - Jigsaw the groups into new groups so that each group has at least one or two representatives for each biography.

   - Let students take turns sharing their information so that all students can benefit.

   - If you desire, let students take notes during their jigsaw groups. They can use column charts to keep track of the information and this can be used as an assessment at the end of the lesson.

Fact Sort *(cont.)*

Procedure *(cont.)*

4. Let students share what they learned about the individuals. List this information on the board under the person's name and picture. This should be the end of a class period.

5. Before the next class period, compile all these facts into one master list, print a copy of this list per group, cut the facts into slips, and put the slips into bags. (You should have one bag per group, each containing the facts you listed, cut into one-fact slips.) Put slips with the names of the individuals into the bags, too. Then, erase the classroom board.

6. At the beginning of the next class period, have students rejoin their groups. Show the bags of disorganized facts and explain that groups will be working to match these facts to the correct people.

7. Give each group a fact bag. Have groups take out the slips with names on them and lay these slips on a desk. Groups will now sort through the remaining facts, putting the appropriate facts under each person's name. Allow time for completion. Do not offer to help students at this point.

8. Reconvene the class. Give each group a roll of clear tape (or a tape dispenser). You will now go around the class asking each group to offer one fact at a time. Groups will start by offering the facts they are fairly certain they have placed correctly. If all groups have placed this fact under the same person, everyone can tape this fact underneath the person's name. If groups have placed the fact under different people, have the class debate where this fact should go before moving it. Eventually, you will have correct facts taped under each person, with only difficult facts remaining. Discuss these difficult facts and work as a class to tape them under the correct people.

9. Have students put their names on the backs of their taped people/facts and have them turn in this work to you.

Fact Sort *(cont.)*

Differentiation Strategies

- **Above grade level**—On the first day of this lesson, encourage groups to brainstorm long lists of facts. Allow enough time for groups to create a list of at least 10–15 facts for the people described in their biographies. Longer lists will make sorting these facts more difficult. Also, on the second day, have groups tape their facts into place before discovering for sure if they are right or wrong. Make this a game and award a point for each correctly placed fact. Offer the winning team a small classroom reward of your choice.

- **Below grade level**—On the first day of this lesson, reduce the number of facts that each group must find. Limit the number of facts you list on your classroom board to no more than five for each of the three people (and make the facts obviously descriptive of the person profiled).

- **English language learners**— Much of this lesson is already accomplished orally. On the lesson's second day, after groups have placed the name headings on desks, pair these students with reading buddies. Choose reading buddies who are strong and encouraging readers. Speak with these strong readers individually and instruct them not to take over the project, but instead to be helpers to their partners.

Assessment

1. Ask each group to find an appropriate number of facts in the written biography. Offer a score from 1–10 for completion (and mark this on your class list). If you like, also offer a quick score for effort and involvement in this first step of the activity.

2. As groups work to match facts to people on the second day of the activity, circulate and offer each student a quick score from 1–10 based on effort and involvement.

3. Assess groups' completed (taped) fact sheets using the *Traits of Good Writing* (page 22) or the assessment strategy of your choice. (After working as a class to place facts, all should be placed correctly and thus most groups should receive high scores.)

Make TIME

Lesson Summary

Students will explore the format of a biography and will then write and illustrate biographies of people they consider heroes for inclusion in a classroom version of TIME Magazine. This is one of the more involved and time-consuming lessons included in this book.

Objectives

- Students will use the general skills and strategies of the writing process.
- Students will understand structural patterns or organization in informational texts (e.g., chronological, logical or sequential order).

Multiple Intelligences

- verbal/linguistic
- intrapersonal
- visual/spatial
- bodily/kinesthetic

Materials

- notebook paper and writing utensils
- blank, white paper
- pens, colored pencils, crayons, markers

Preparation

1. Choose three TIME biographies and copy them for your students. (Each student should have one copy of a TIME biography to use as a reference.)

2. Make a class list to use with the assessment.

Procedure

1. Explore each of this lesson's three TIME biographies using the following procedure.

   - Display a TIME cover. (Each image is on the CD if you want to show them to the class using a projection system.)

   - Ask students what they already know about this person.

   - Then, read aloud the accompanying biography. As you read, encourage students to take notes of the things they think are important.

2. Write the person's name on your classroom board and ask your class to share the things that are important about this person.

   - Repeat this procedure with this lesson's remaining people.

3. Look at the lists you created. Then, ask your students to find partners and write five questions that every biography must answer. Let students share their questions. Write the most popular ones on the board and leave them posted for future use.

Make TIME *(cont.)*

Procedure *(cont.)*

4. Explain that students will now be choosing heroes and will be writing and illustrating biographies of these people in the format of TIME Magazine. To do so, students will be using the writing process. When finished, you will combine these biographies into a classroom version of TIME Magazine.

5. The first step of the writing process is prewriting. Have each student choose a person about whom he or she would like to write. Define the guidelines for your students—Will you have your class research and write about famous heroes such as Martin Luther King Jr.? Will they write biographies of parents, coaches, or other people they know? Will they write biographies of friends?

6. Once students have chosen people to profile, have students reflect on the necessary information that must be included in a biography. Talk about these as a class. Remind students to include information that answers the five questions listed on the classroom board. These are the five questions that every biography must answer. This step may or may not include research.

7. The next step of the writing process is drafting. Have students include answers to the five prewriting questions in their drafted biographies. Allow appropriate time for completion. This may take a full class period.

8. Next, students will revise their work. Have students pass their drafts to editing partners, who will offer three positive comments and one suggestion for revision (or have students complete a revision strategy of your choice).

9. Students should now edit their work, looking for spelling and grammatical errors. At the end of this step, students should have thoroughly marked drafts—the messier, the better!

10. As part of the publishing process, have each student draw a full-page, color illustration of their person. On the backs of these illustrations, have students write final versions of their hero biographies. Have students leave margins on the left sides of their work to make binding possible.

11. Collect students' written and illustrated biographies and bind them together into a class version of TIME Magazine. If you like, allow early finishers to design the cover.

Make TIME *(cont.)*

Differentiation Strategies

- **Above grade level**—Let these students who usually finish early include a few other creative details in their biographies. Tell them to imagine that they could have dinner with these people. What are the five questions they would each ask this person? Have them include this information in their biographies or have them write fictional accounts of meeting these people.

- **Below grade level**—Have students profile people they know well (parents, grandparents, teachers, friends, coaches, etc.). This removes the need for research. Extend the time students may use to answer the five questions in the prewriting stage and offer help as needed. Consider skipping the revision step of the writing process.

- **English language learners**—Have these students record their answers to the five questions on an audiotape. Have each student draw an illustration of his or her person on the back of this sheet. These are their finished products. If you like, have students present their people and recordings to the class.

Assessment

1. As students are working on their biographies, circulate and offer quick scores from 1–10 based on effort and involvement.

2. Assess finished biographies using the *Traits of Good Writing* or the writing assessment strategy of your choice. (As this lesson includes a complete pass through the writing process, it is appropriate to use the language arts assessment strategy recommended by your school or district.)

Traits of Good Writing include:

- Ideas that are interesting and important

- Ideas that are at the heart of the piece

- Organization that is logical and effective

- Voice that is individual and appropriate

- Word choice that is specific and memorable

- Sentence fluency that is smooth and expressive

- Conventions that are correct and communicative

Choose Your Own Adventure

Lesson Summary

In this relatively advanced lesson, students will explore selected biographies before writing choose-your-own-adventure stories based on these people. What could these people's lives—and the world—have been like if they had made alternate decisions?

Objectives

- Students will use the general skills and strategies of the writing process.

- Students will contribute to group discussions.

Multiple Intelligences

- interpersonal

- logical/mathematical

- verbal/linguistic

Materials

- blank paper, writing utensils

- illustration supplies including colored pens, pencils, crayons, etc.

Preparation

1. Choose various TIME biographies and copy them for your students. (Each group of students will need one TIME biography.)

2. Organize blank white paper and illustration supplies.

3. Make copies of the assessment rubric in the assessment section to grade students' work.

Procedure

1. Discuss the decisions that famous people have needed to make. What decisions has the president of the United States faced? What decisions have athletes or musicians faced?

2. Explain that students will be working in groups to read a biography and list decisions that each person faced. (Choose the number of decisions that students need to include.)

3. Split students into groups (3–4 students works well for this lesson) and give each group a copy of one of this lesson's written biographies. Allow time for groups to read the biographies and make lists of their person's decisions. Offer help, as needed.

4. Once all groups are finished, reconvene the class and discuss students' findings. On the classroom board, list the people and the decisions each had to make. Work together to come up with a creative and interesting list of decisions—the longer the list, the better.

Choose Your Own Adventure *(cont.)*

Procedure *(cont.)*

5. Using a few of these decisions, discuss what the person's life and consequently the world might be like if he or she had decided differently. How do the decisions made by these people shape students' lives? (This may be the end of a class period.)

6. Next, explain that each small group will be choosing one of these people to use in a choose-your-own-adventure story. (If they like, they can choose someone other than the person whose biography they had initially.) Follow this procedure:

    *   Groups will use blank paper and illustrate their stories.

    *   Groups should choose a person and then choose the decisions from the lists on your classroom board. Assign the number of decisions that they must choose.

    *   Each group's choose-your-own-adventure story should generally follow the selected person's life. Students should describe how the person grew up. They should feel free to fictionalize, when necessary, but should also include as many facts as possible.

*   When a group's subject reaches a decision (from the list on your classroom board), the student writers will offer readers the same choice and then direct readers to one of two pages, where readers can find the outcomes of their choices. The correct decision will lead deeper into the story. The other choice will result in an ending of some sort (good or bad). Because in real life, the subject made only one choice, groups will have to infer and make up what might have happened if the subject had chosen differently.

*   The end of the story will be the subject's real-life outcome.

7. Allow appropriate time for groups to write and illustrate their choose-your-own-adventure stories. (This might take up to three class periods.)

8. When finished, have groups share their stories with the rest of the class. If you like, have groups read aloud their stories and allow the audience to make decisions.

Choose Your Own Adventure *(cont.)*

Differentiation Strategies

- **Above grade level**—Increase the number of decisions each character in the choose-your-own-adventure stories needs to make. If you like, allow groups to follow "incorrect" decisions past a simple ending (offering additional choices that may lead to dead ends or even lead back to the correct flow of events). Another alternative is to have these students write the endings that are fictionalized. The other students can write the true stories.

- **Below grade level**—This is a difficult lesson. To make it easier, reduce the number of decisions in each choose-your-own-adventure story (maybe only two decisions, total). Define ahead of time (as a class) the two decisions each character will face in students' books and, perhaps, the outcomes of these decisions. Have reluctant writers present their stories orally to the class, using pictures as visual aides.

- **English language learners**—To make it a bit easier, have students illustrate and caption their choose-your-own-adventure stories, but do not insist that they write the entire story in paragraph form.

Assessment

1. Use the following assessment to grade students' written work.

   > **1 = weak**
   > **3 = average**
   > **5 = strong**

   - Grabs the audience's attention

   - Writes with main idea and supporting details

   - Contains enough background information so that readers can understand the story

   - Uses sensory descriptions in writing

   - Is neat and organized

   - Followed directions

Talking Hands

Lesson Summary

Students will research and present information about selected biographies. Next, small groups will make posters of these people and label them with information about what these people did (hands), felt (heart), said (mouth), and experienced (eyes).

Objectives

- Students will use strategies to edit and publish written work (e.g., selects presentation format according to purpose, incorporates illustrations).

- Students will organize ideas for oral presentation (e.g., uses notes or other memory aids, organizes ideas around major points).

Multiple Intelligences

- interpersonal
- bodily/kinesthetic

Materials

- large paper or poster board
- pens, crayons, markers

Preparation

1. Select three biographies and make three copies of each one for a total of nine copies. There will be one copy for each of the nine groups. (Three groups will have the same biography.)

2. Copy the assessment rubric at the end of the lesson, one for each group.

Procedure

1. Split your class into nine small groups.

2. Explain that each group will be exploring a biography and writing four facts about the person. With nine groups total, three groups will represent the same biography.

3. Give each group a copy of one of the biographies and allow appropriate time for groups to read the material and write four facts.

4. Next, explain that small groups will be working with the other group(s) that studied the same person to organize a short presentation for the rest of the class. The presentations should be in the following format:

   - One student should start by offering the class a quick overview of his or her person. What is the person's name and what is he or she best known for?

   - In turn, each remaining student in the group should offer one fact.

   - To close, one student should tell the class how this person has been important to people who followed and to the world.

Talking Hands *(cont.)*

Procedure *(cont.)*

5. Allow large groups a couple of minutes to organize their presentations.

6. While groups are presenting, display the appropriate TIME cover. (Each image is on the CD if you want to show them to the class using a projection system.)

7. Explain that the original small groups will now be reconvening to make posters showing information about any one of these people (each group may choose its favorite). The posters will take the following format:

   - An illustration of the person that takes almost the entire poster page.

   - Arrows to text that students will write describing what the person *did* (hands), *felt* (heart), *said* (mouth) and *experienced* (eyes).

   - Students' names on the back.

8. Gauge your class level and offer examples and additional directions for the posters as necessary. This might include working as a class to make an example based on a famous person whom the students know.

9. Allow appropriate time for groups to complete their posters.

10. Display finished posters in your room.

Talking Hands *(cont.)*

Differentiation Strategies

- **Above grade level**—Have these students add the following additional piece of information to their posters. Ask them, *What would this person do if given the opportunity?* Let them decide where on the body this piece of information should go.

- **Below grade level**—Display the TIME cover and read the biographies aloud as a group. Stop frequently to answer the students' questions. Also, make sure small groups understand the poster requirements before allowing them to start drawing. Give them a clear rubric. You might solidify the directions by creating an example as a class.

- **English language learners**—Consider having students geographically represent all elements of this lesson. For example, instead of using words to describe what the person on their poster experienced, ask students to represent it with illustrations, or have them act it out for the class.

Assessment

1. The initial small groups (Steps 1–3) will each write four facts about the person they study. On your class list, quickly give each student a score from 1–4 (one point for every fact) based on completion.

2. As the large groups present the people they studied (Steps 4–6), use your class list to give each student a quick score from 1–3 based on effort and participation.

3. Use the following rubric for grading the posters.

   1 = weak
   2 = average
   3 = strong

   - The poster has all the information required.

   - The poster is neat and easy to read.

   - The poster is colorful and creative.

   - Spelling and punctuation are correct.

   - The poster shows that the students understand the topic.

A Complete Person

Lesson Summary

After exploring the biographies, pairs of students will each research an aspect of one of these persons' lives (background, key dates, achievements, death, fun fact). Students will then collaborate to organize and present all the information about their people. This lesson requires that students do research.

Objectives

- Students will use a variety of strategies to plan research (e.g., organizes prior knowledge about a topic, develops a course of action, determines how to locate necessary information).

- Students will make basic oral presentations to the class (e.g., includes content appropriate to the audience, incorporates several sources of information).

Multiple Intelligences

- verbal/linguistic
- interpersonal

Materials

- paper and writing utensils
- age–appropriate research materials including encyclopedias or Internet

Preparation

1. Choose three TIME biographies and copy them for your students. (Each pair of students will need one of these TIME biographies.)

2. Make a class list to use with the assessment.

Procedure

1. Preview the biographies you selected using the following technique:

   - Display one TIME cover. (Each image is on the CD if you want to show them to the class using a projection system.)

   - Ask students what they know about this person.

   - What clues does the TIME cover offer to help students extend this background knowledge? What can they discover from this document? (Look at clothing, text, symbols, etc.)

   - What do students think they will find out when they read about this person?

   - Read the corresponding biography aloud, pausing after each paragraph or section to ask students what they learned from the reading. Continue this until you have finished reading the page.

   - Repeat this procedure with this lesson's remaining two people.

A Complete Person *(cont.)*

Procedure *(cont.)*

2. Explain that pairs of students will now research one aspect of one of these people. Make sure you have 15 groups. This might mean that some students work alone (your above-grade-level students) and others will work with partners. Assign one topic and one biography to each group. You will need 15 groups to research the following five topics for each of the three biographies:

   - Background
   - Key dates
   - Achievements
   - Death
   - Fun facts

3. Allow appropriate time for students to research and write at least one paragraph about their topics.

4. Explain that everyone who researched the same person will be collaborating on a presentation for the class. Groups will put together all the information they found (background, key dates, achievements, death, or fun facts).

5. Allow time for groups to organize and practice their presentations. If time allows, have fast finishers create visual aides to use with their presentations.

6. Have each large group present its information. Be sure to define audience expectations including respectful listening, questions at the end, applause, or other classroom audience procedures.

A Complete Person *(cont.)*

Differentiation Strategies

- **Above grade level**—Have students replace *death* and *key dates* with *lasting influence* and *evidence of courage* in the list of research topics for each biography.

- **Below grade level**—The easiest "job" in this lesson is researching key dates as they are given in the accompanying biography materials. Consider asking these students to complete this job and if they have additional time, to also illustrate these key dates. Consider pre-planning websites that students can use for research and writing specific directions explaining where students can find the information they need.

- **English language learners**—Consider pairing English language learners with motivated helpers or volunteers. This activity provides an opportunity for your English language learners to establish working friendships in the classroom. If you are working with a full class of English language learners, consider limiting research to the biographies included in this book, and offer help reading these aloud as needed.

Assessment

1. As pairs are researching their facts, circulate and give each student a quick score from 1–10 based on effort and participation.

2. As large groups present their information, assign each student up to 15 points based on involvement, relevance of researched material, and presentation skills.

Time Line Game

Lesson Summary

In this fun game, after exploring the selected biographies, groups will create lists of important events in the lives of these three people. Students will then trade lists with other groups and will have to use the knowledge they remember from the initial exploration to put the important events in order. The winning group earns a reward of your choice.

Objectives

- Students will summarize and paraphrase information in texts.
- Students will use prewriting strategies to plan written work (e.g., brainstorms).

Multiple Intelligences

- verbal/linguistic
- interpersonal
- logical/mathematical

Materials

- notebook paper and writing utensils
- note cards
- white sticker labels

Preparation

1. Choose three TIME biographies. Make enough copies so that each student has one to reference.

2. Copy rubric in the assessment section. Also, make a class list to use with the assessment.

Procedure

1. Preview the biographies of three different individuals using the following technique:

   - Give students copies of the TIME covers. Each student should only have one cover, but there will be three different covers distributed in the class.

   - Let students use white sticker labels or draw their own caption bubbles. Tell the class to write what they think these people might say to the class if given the chance.

   - Encourage students to look for clues on the TIME covers. (Look at clothing, text, symbols, etc.)

   - Let students share their captions with other students around their seats. If time permits, let some share their captions with the class.

   - Then, read all three background accounts to the class. After each one, pause and ask the students if they think their captions could be correct now that they know the background information.

Time Line Game *(cont.)*

Procedure *(cont.)*

2. Explain that students will now be working in groups to create time lines for these three people. Each group will be responsible for creating one time line with the relevant dates listed and will then write each event on separate note cards without including the dates.

3. Split the class into three equal groups (teams). Assign each group one of the people from this lesson. The subject can be the same person that they wrote the caption for. Each student in each group will need to find one important date that relates to his or her person. Depending on the time you choose to use with this activity, you can ask students to get their events (and dates) directly from the accompanying biographical material, or you can allow time for research using encyclopedias, the Internet, or other appropriate sources.

4. Allow students/teams time to research and write their time lines. Remind students that each team will need a time line that includes dates and events (this serves as an answer key) and will also need to list each event on separate note cards without the date.

5. Reconvene the class. Have groups turn in their time lines (answer keys) and then pass their note cards to another group.

6. Explain the following rules of the time line game:

   - Each student will be responsible for one note card and will carry this card with himself or herself throughout the game.

   - Each group's goal is for everyone to line up with the events in the correct chronological order.

   - The game will go in turns: each group will line up (with note cards in hand), doing its best to put the events in order, and then the teacher will look at the time line answer key and tell the group how many events are in the correct order (but not which ones are out of order). Encourage students to draw on the knowledge they remember from the initial exploration of these people.

   - After the groups have lined up once and heard how many spots are correct, they can adjust their positions as they think fit.

   - The group that lines up in the correct order and taking the least number of turns, wins a classroom reward of your choice.

Time Line Game *(cont.)*

Differentiation Strategies

- **Above grade level**—Explain ahead of time that groups will be trying to put other groups' events in order and encourage students to find unusual, interesting, or obscure facts that they think will stump other teams. Make sure these students trade cards with other groups that have a more challenging time line.

- **Below grade level**—Have students work in pairs (within groups) to list one event between them. This will cut down on the overall number of events that will be part of the time line game.

- **English language learners**—Have students illustrate the events they find and write phrases rather than sentences about the events on a time line and note cards. As these students work to place the cards in correct order, read the fact aloud for this group. Or, if these students are heterogenously grouped, pair them with reading buddies.

Assessment

1. While students are working in groups, circulate and give each student up to five points for participation and up to five points for finding and listing a relevant time line event. Answer the following with a yes or no. Give 5 points for each *yes*, 0 points for *no*.

   - Is the time line neat and easy to read?

   - Are the punctuation and grammar correct?

   - Does the time line show an understanding of the topic?

   - Does the time line have accurate information?

   - Does the time line meet the requirements of the assignment?

2. During the game, assess students based on effort and participation.

Change the World

Lesson Summary

After reading selected biographies, each student will choose one of these people as the subject for a poster showing what the world was like before this person was born and what it is like now (highlighting how each person changed the world).

Objectives

- Students will use strategies to edit and publish written work (e.g. incorporates information, shares finished product).

- Students will summarize and paraphrase information in texts.

Multiple Intelligences

- verbal/linguistic

- intrapersonal

- bodily/kinesthetic

Materials

- notebook paper and writing utensils

- large paper or poster board

- pens, crayons, markers

Preparation

1. Choose three TIME biographies and copy them for your students. (Students will be working in groups of three students each, and each student in the group should have a different TIME biography.)

2. Make a class list to use with the assessment.

3. Copy the rubric in the assessment section to grade students' posters.

Procedure

1. Place students in groups of three. Give each student a different copy of one TIME biography. There will be three different biographies per group.

2. Explain that students will be working independently to read the biographies and then write on the backs of the photocopied sheets one way each person changed the world. Prompt students by asking, *How did this person change the world?*

3. Allow appropriate time for each student to read his or her biography and write on the back one way this person changed the world.

4. Tell students they will now be passing their sheets to other students in their groups. Students should complete the same procedure: read the new biography and write on the back one way this person changed the world. There is one catch—students cannot duplicate what they have already written about the other biography and must find another way this person influenced the world.

Change the World *(cont.)*

Procedure *(cont.)*

5. Repeat Step 4. At the end of this step, every student should have read all three TIME biographies and each TIME biography should have three ways this person changed the world written on the back.

6. Have students return the original biographies to one another in their groups. Tell students they will now be making posters about these people. Each student's poster will show two versions of the world—one before the person he or she choose was born and a second version showing the change(s) this person created. (Depending on your class level, require students to illustrate one to three changes.)

7. Show students where they can find poster supplies and allow appropriate time for students to complete their posters.

8. If you like, have students present their posters to the class, describing the changes they illustrated. Display these posters around the classroom or in the hallways so that others can appreciate the changes these individuals brought to our world today.

Change the World *(cont.)*

Differentiation Strategies

- **Above grade level**—Have these students choose the most important change from the back of each biography in their group. These students can also decide which person had the biggest influence. During their presentations, let these students explain their reasoning. If others in the group disagree, let them justify their reasons for disagreement.

- **Below grade level**—Stop after students have explored the first biography. Display the TIME covers and offer quick (recap) biographies for each of this lesson's three people. Discuss with your class the changes these people have created. Making a chart that records important changes for this group would also be helpful. Then, have students make posters showing the one change they think is the most important.

- **English language learners**—Depending on their ability levels, these students can illustrate, compose phrases, or write simple sentences instead of lengthy explanations.

Assessment

1. During the reading and listing part of the activity, walk around the room assessing students as they work. You can record this assessment on a class list. Be sure to stop and assist those who need extra help.

2. Grade students' posters using the following rubric.

   > 1 = **weak**
   > 2 = **average**
   > 3 = **strong**

   - The student followed directions.

   - The poster is nicely organized and easy to understand.

   - The artwork on the poster is appropriate.

   - Spelling and punctuation (if any) on the poster are accurate.

   - The poster shows that the student understood the information.

TIME Cover

Lesson Summary

Students will use the techniques of primary source document exploration to search for information in TIME covers and will then create their own magazine covers, hiding as many information clues as possible.

Objectives

- Students will understand the use and meaning of symbols and images in visual media (e.g., the dependence of symbols on shared social and cultural understandings).

- Students will use the general skills and strategies of the writing process.

Multiple Intelligences

- verbal/linguistic
- interpersonal
- logical/mathematical

Materials

- one copy of any TIME cover not used in this lesson (All TIME covers are on the CD if you want to display the cover using a projection system.)
- notebook paper and writing utensils
- large paper or poster board
- colored pencils, pens, crayons, markers

Preparation

1. Copy one TIME cover to use as an example with the entire class.

2. Copy three TIME covers that you desire to use for this lesson. (Each group of students will need one biography.)

3. Make a class list to use with the assessment. Also, make copies of the rubric in the assessment section.

Procedure

1. Tell students that they are archaeologists, like Indiana Jones, who have stumbled upon three artifacts from an unknown culture. They will be examining these artifacts for clues that give information about the people shown and also about the culture.

2. Display the one TIME cover not related to this lesson.

3. Work with students to explore this document for clues. Who is this person? How can you tell? Look at how he or she is dressed and at any jewelry or other styling. Explore the background for clues. What do students think this person is famous for? Are there text clues? Was this person rich or poor, a government leader, or a sports hero? Help students make an educated guess as to who this person is based on the clues they discover.

TIME Cover *(cont.)*

Procedure *(cont.)*

4. Choose three TIME covers for this lesson. Split students into small groups (3–4 students per group work well for this lesson) and explain that each group will be performing this same exploration with one of the three "artifacts" (TIME covers) from this lesson. After they discover as many clues as possible, they will make a presentation to the class describing their guess as to who this person was/is (and explaining how they came to this guess). If you like, define the number of clues that each group must find.

5. Give each group a TIME cover (without biography) and allow time for groups to explore this cover as a primary source document and to list the clues they find. As groups start to finish, encourage them to organize and practice their presentations to the class. The presentations should answer the following question: *What do you know about this person's life and how do you know it?*

6. Have groups present their covers and guesses to the class, focusing on what clues they found and what they think these clues mean. After groups have presented, discuss these people and try to come to a class consensus as to who they think each of these people is/was.

7. Read aloud the TIME biographies, emphasizing students' correct and incorrect guesses about the person. Praise the amounts of information students were able to find in documents that, on the surface, initially looked rather basic.

8. Explain that students will now be creating their own "artifacts," which will take the format of magazine covers. They may choose any people they like to immortalize on their covers, and will then hide as many information clues as possible. For example, if they choose a football player, they might illustrate the person resting a hand on a football. Or, if they choose a politician, they might show the person looking presidential and poised. If you like, define the number of clues students must hide in their covers.

9. Have students trade covers, seeing if they can discover the clues the other students hid.

10. Let students present their magazine covers to the class, identifying and describing the person and then explaining their clues.

TIME Cover *(cont.)*

Differentiation Strategies

- **Above grade level**—This lesson is open-ended and these students can elaborate to their hearts' desires on the work. Have them include more clues on their magazine covers. If you like, have students research the people they decide to put on their covers and have them present their TIME covers as the focal points of larger hero reports.

- **Below grade level**—Reduce the number of clues for which each group is responsible while exploring the published TIME cover and while making their own covers. Have an aid work with these students to organize their clues and give them added support.

- **English language learners**—This is a strong activity to use with English language learners because many of the elements are visual rather than written. Because of this lesson's built-in appropriateness for English language learners, you may choose to extend the time you take with this activity, asking English language learners to explore all three TIME covers for hidden clues (as suggested for above-grade-level students). In the second half of the activity, make sure your English language learners choose people for their own TIME covers, whom they know well, thus removing the need for text-based research.

Assessment

1. While groups are exploring the published TIME covers, circulate and give each student a score from 1–10 based on effort and involvement.

2. Collect groups' finished magazine covers and assess them using the following rubric.

   1 = poor
   2 = good
   3 = strong

   - The cover meets the requirements of the assignment.

   - The content is accurate.

   - The content shows that students understood the researched information.

   - The student effectively presented the magazine cover to the class.

Fun Facts Game

Lesson Summary

Each student will research one fun fact about a selected individual. After making a list of these facts and then cutting them into slips, students will play a version of the game Balderdash® in which they compete to guess true facts while making up untrue ones to trick their classmates.

Objectives

- Students will use a variety of strategies to plan research (e.g., develops a course of action, determines how to locate necessary information).

- Students will make basic oral presentations to the class (e.g., uses subject-related information and vocabulary).

Multiple Intelligences

- verbal/linguistic
- interpersonal

Materials

- notebook paper and writing utensils
- small plastic bags
- note cards
- large paper or poster board
- pens, crayons, markers

Preparation

1. Choose three different TIME biographies and make copies for the class. (Each student needs only one TIME biography copy.)

2. Make copies of the scoring rubric in the assessment section, one for each student. Also, be sure to share this rubric with students before they begin writing their note cards so they understand the expectations.

Procedure

1. Divide the class into three groups with equal numbers of students in each group.

2. In each group, assign an equal number of students to research one of the individuals. For example, three students will research one person, three students will research another person, and three other students will research a different person. Give each student a written biography of the person he or she is researching.

3. Allow students an appropriate amount of time to read their biographies and to each write one fact about their person on note cards. Encourage students to discover obscure, creative, or fun facts—ones they think are amazing enough to potentially be fiction!

4. Have students write their names on the backs of the cards and turn them in to you. Keep groups' facts separated from other groups' by storing them in small plastic bags.

5. Explain that students will later be using these facts to play a game. But first, you will be exploring these three people as a class. The more students can remember about these people from the class discussion, the better they will do in the game that follows.

Fun Facts Game *(cont.)*

Procedure *(cont.)*

6. Preview the biographies using the following technique:

   - Display the three TIME covers. (Each image is on the CD if you want to show them to the class using a projection system.)

   - Place students back into their three large groups. Have students in each group read one biography and then talk about what they learned from the reading. What was interesting about this person's life?

   - Then, jigsaw the groups making sure that several people from each group are mixed together.

   - Let students take turns talking about each biography. They should share what they learned and talk about what makes this person interesting. This way, all the students get the benefit of learning without having to read each biography.

7. Explain that it is now time to play the game. Students will be making three-person teams within their initial groups. These teams will be competing with the rest of the group in a version of the game Balderdash®. Tell students the following rules:

   - One team will pick a slip from the plastic bag of note card facts.

   - The team will then have exactly three minutes to write two additional but false "facts" on this card. These facts should be believable because the teams want to trick one another.

   - When three minutes are up, the team will read all three "facts" to the other teams in the group. The other teams will vote for the one fact they think is true.

   - If a team guesses the true fact, it earns one point. Every incorrect guess earns the team that wrote the fake fact a point.

   - Continue taking turns around the group until all fact note cards are used up, or until a designated time expires.

   - The team in each group with the most points will earn a classroom reward of your choice.

8. Give each group a small plastic bag of facts—not the ones they initially wrote! Allow an appropriate amount of time for students to play the fun fact game. Reward the winners.

Fun Facts Game *(cont.)*

Differentiation Strategies

- **Above grade level**—Encourage students to find fun facts outside the written biographies that accompany this lesson. Allow them to use age-appropriate resource materials such as the school library or the Internet. With this in mind, students should be able to find much "wackier" facts—ones that will be more fun to use with the game!

- **Below grade level**—Put students in teams of three and then make each team of three (instead of every student) responsible for writing a fun fact on a note card. This will decrease your overall number of facts and will thus shorten the fun fact game.

- **English language learners**—Have these students work with buddies who are proficient in English to read the biographies and write the false facts on note cards. Instruct these buddies to work with these students and slowly explain the steps they are taking. If extra assistance is needed, instruct these students to notify the teacher.

Assessment

1. On your class list, check off each student as they turn in a note card fact. Assign an appropriate number of points to this task. For example, give the assignment 12 points. Use the scoring provided to decide on a grade.

   1 = did not meet expectations
   2 = met expectations
   3 = exceeded expectations

- Did the student follow directions?

- Are the false statements believable?

- Do students include information from at least two different sources?

- Are the grammar, spelling, and punctuation correct on the note cards?

Math Word Problems

Lesson Summary

After exploring the selected biographies, students will work in pairs to write math word problems about these people. Groups can choose to present their word problems to the class, preferably during the math portion of the day.

Objectives

- Students will use strategies (e.g., adapts organization, form) to write for a variety of purposes.
- Students will organize ideas for oral presentations (e.g., uses notes or other memory aids).

Multiple Intelligences

- verbal/linguistic
- logical/mathematical
- interpersonal

Materials

- notebook paper and writing utensils
- large paper
- markers

Preparation

1. Choose three different TIME biographies. Divide the class into three equal groups. Copy a different TIME biography for each group. Make sure that each student has his or her own copy of the biography.

2. Make a class list to use with the assessment.

Procedure

1. Explore the biographies using the following technique:

   - Split the class into three groups, with each group responsible for organizing a presentation about a different person.

   - Designate a leader for each group.

   - Have each group read aloud its biography. Students can take turns reading, read silently, or read with partners.

   - Explain that groups will now be organizing presentations that will explain their people to the rest of the class. These presentations should include quick overviews (given by the group leader), followed by one important fact given by each remaining group member.

   - While groups present their people, display the appropriate TIME cover. Each image is on the CD if you want to show them to the class using a projection system.

2. Commend groups on their presentations and explain the second half of this activity, in which students will be working with partners to create math word problems that relate to one of these people.

Math Word Problems *(cont.)*

Procedure *(cont.)*

3. Give each pair of students a copy of its chosen biography and time line and explain the following procedure.

- Each pair should scan its biography, looking for the potential for numbers. This might be as easy as exploring the time line, or might be more creative, such as realizing that amounts of money may have something to do with the person. Again, encourage students to first look for instances of numbers in these biographies, without yet worrying exactly how they will use these numbers in word problems. Have students keep a list of these possible numbers.

- As pairs finish their lists of possible numbers, ask them to conference with you before starting to write their math word problems. In these short conferences, brainstorm with students how they might use the numbers they found in math word problems. Be creative! If students get stuck, try prompting them with questions such as: *What do these numbers mean? What could you add? What could you subtract? What could you multiply? What could you divide?* If you like, require students to include in their word problems operations you are currently studying in math class.

- Each pair will be responsible for writing one word problem.

- After a pair meets with you to solidify the basics of its problem, allow the pair to start writing a math word problem. If time allows, have the pair write a draft before writing a published copy. Tell students to solve their math problems to make sure they work!

4. Have each group present its math problems to the class using markers on large sheets of paper. These can be hung at the front of class and students can work out the problem on their own papers. Have the class do a certain number of these problems as a math assignment.

Math Word Problems *(cont.)*

Differentiation Strategies

- **Above grade level**—Encourage these students to include more difficult operations in their math word problems, or encourage students to write multistep problems. If time permits, include each pair's problem in a "math book" assignment, which you can photocopy and distribute to the class.

- **Below grade level**—Read aloud a biography unrelated to this lesson and demonstrate how you can find numbers in the text. Work with your class to use these numbers in math word problems, demonstrating the procedure until your class seems comfortable. Only then, allow them to write their own math word problems based on this lesson's biographies.

- **English language learners**— Depending on the level of your English language learners, either have them illustrate math problems (writing only the formula and answer), or have them illustrate the problems and write short captions underneath. If time permits, work with these students to construct word problems based on the information they provided.

Assessment

1. As groups present biographies (at the end of Step 1 in this activity), assess these presentations based on the following.

   1 = did not meet expectations
   2 = met expectations
   3 = exceeded expectations

   - Organization
   - Participation
   - Presentation skills

2. When pairs conference with you (in the middle of Step 3 in this activity), put a check next to the students' names on your class list. Assign this task an appropriate number of points.

3. Offer a small amount of extra credit to pairs willing to present their finished math word problems to the class.

4. Collect finished word problems and assess them using the *Traits of Good Writing* (page 22), or with a rubric that rewards the expository writing skills of clarity and sentence fluency as well as the mathematics behind the problem. Or, use the assessment strategy of your choice.

Skits

Lesson Summary

Students will work in groups to write and present skits based on the lives of several individuals.

Objectives

- Students will make basic oral presentations to the class (e.g., relates ideas and observations, incorporates visual aids or props, incorporates several sources of information).

- Students will use prewriting strategies to plan written work (e.g., uses graphic organizers, groups related ideas).

Multiple Intelligences

- verbal/linguistic
- interpersonal
- bodily/kinesthetic

Materials

- notebook paper and writing utensils

Preparation

1. Divide students into groups (five students in each group). Choose enough TIME biographies so that each group can have a different one. Copy the biographies.

2. Make a class list to use with the assessment.

3. Copy the rubric in the assessment section to score each of the plays.

Procedure

1. Divide students into groups and give each group copies of one of this lesson's TIME biographies.

2. Explain that each group will be writing and presenting a skit based on its person's life. They will use the following procedure:

   - Before groups may start writing their actual scripts, they should make lists of the characters their plays will include and lists of scenes they plan to write. Explain that scenes might include reenactments of their persons' childhoods, early struggles, major achievements, and later lives. (In fact, you may require that groups write four-scene plays, using this sequence.) Their finished plays will present these scenes in order.

   - Allow each group time to read its TIME biography and create a character and scene list. (This may take an entire class period.)

Skits *(cont.)*

Procedure *(cont.)*

- After the groups have written outlines, they should start writing their skits' scripts. Depending on your class level and the time you allow for this activity, written scripts can be detailed assignments using the steps of the writing process, or you can allow groups to rehearse their plays without actually writing anything down.

- Have groups check their scripts with you before starting to rehearse their plays. Make sure you split groups into defined areas of the room, hallway, outside, or other available space to allow room for noisy rehearsals.

- Once groups are finished rehearsing their skits, have them perform their skits for the class. Be sure to define audience expectations including respectful listening and applause at the end of each skit. As groups perform, display the appropriate TIME cover. (All images are included on the CD if you want to show them to your class using a projection system.)

3. Collect finished scripts.

4. Close the activity with a discussion of these people:

   - Which of these three people do students think faced the most difficult struggle?

   - Which of these people do students think had the most lasting impact?

   - Who would students most like to be? Who would they least like to be?

   - Which one scene in any of these plays did students find the most exciting?

Skits *(cont.)*

Differentiation Strategies

- **Above grade level**—Increase the number of scenes that skits must include. Make students responsible for brainstorming and defining these scenes (instead of offering the requirements of childhood, major achievements, etc.). Depending on the time you allow for this activity, ask students to create costumes, props, and sets.

- **Below grade level**—Define jobs for students within their groups. One should be the director, another should be in charge of the script, another should be in charge of creating costumes (using classroom art supplies), and another should be the lead actor. Consider asking your more artistic students to create costumes, your motivated writers to be in charge of the script, your natural leaders to be directors, and your hams to be actors.

- **English language learners**—Explore each of this lesson's three people as a class, making lists of scenes in these people's lives. Leave these scenes written on your classroom board. When groups make their skits, ask them to use the given scenes as a framework. Reduce requirements for written work, allowing groups to practice and perform their skits without writing a script.

Assessment

1. While groups are working on their scenes and character lists, walk through the room giving each student a score from 1–10 based on effort and participation.

2. Repeat the previous assessment while groups are writing their scripts.

3. Score the skits using the following rubric. Each statement is worth 10 points, giving a possible maximum score of 50.

   - The skit has the correct amount of scenes.

   - The skit accurately shows the individual's life.

   - Every group member participated in the skit.

   - The presentation shows that students understand the individual.

   - The presentation is informative.

Biography Role-Play

Lesson Summary

Each student will "become" a famous individual from history and will answer prearranged questions. Depending on the time allocated to this activity, students can ask one another questions, or you can ask another class, parents, or the community to interact with your in-character students.

Objectives

- Students will organize ideas for oral presentations (e.g., uses notes or other memory aids, organizes ideas around major points, uses traditional structures such as posing and answering a question).

- Students will write in response to literature (e.g., summarizes main ideas and significant details).

Multiple Intelligences

- verbal/linguistic
- intrapersonal
- bodily/kinesthetic

Materials

- writing utensils
- 3 note cards per student

Preparation

1. Choose various TIME biographies and copy them for your students. (Each student should have one biography, but multiple students can have the same biography.)

2. Make a class list to use with the assessment.

Procedure

1. Explore the biographies of the selected individuals using the following technique:

   - Display one TIME cover. (Each image is on the CD if you want to show them to the class using a projection system.)

   - Ask students to imagine they are this person. Then, have students tell the class something about their lives as this famous individual. Encourage students to look at the cover to help them with ideas. Their clothing, text, and symbols can give great clues to the personality of this person.

   - Have students read their biographies with partners. Partners can read it at the same time to improve fluency or they can take turns reading paragraphs.

   - After reading, ask students what they learned about this person. Create a large chart at the front of the room for each biography. Have partners write two facts they learned from the reading. Instruct the class that they may not copy anything already written on the chart paper. They must write something new.

   - Take the time to read each fact aloud to the class. This way, all students can benefit from the biographies that they have not read.

Biography Role-Play *(cont.)*

Procedure *(cont.)*

2. Explain that each student will now be choosing one of these people to study in depth. Students may choose the person they wrote about or they may want to learn about one of the other individuals. If all students gravitate toward one biography, you may need to assign people for students to study.

3. Explain that each student will be researching his or her person and must be able to answer the following questions from memory: When was the person born? When did he or she die? What was this person best known for? What impact did this person have on the world?

4. In addition, each student should write three more questions, each on a note card, which he or she can answer from memory.

5. Give each student a copy of his or her chosen biography and allow time for students to answer the three given questions and to write their three additional note card questions. Depending on your class level and the time you allocate to this activity, you may encourage students to use additional age-appropriate research materials including encyclopedias, the school library, and the Internet.

6. Each student should now have memorized answers to six questions: the three given and the three on their note cards. Depending on the time you allow for this activity, use one of the following three procedures:

- **Option 1:** Have half the class be "askers" and the other half role-play their characters. The askers should wander the room, while the characters hand them the cards so they know what questions to ask. Have askers and characters switch jobs after a given amount of time.

- **Option 2:** Invite parents or another class to tour your biography museum. As these guests enter the room, encourage them to interact with your students (in character) and to ask your students both the given questions and the questions on students' note cards. (Students should hand guests their note cards so their guests have a choice of appropriate questions.) It's fun to have students dress up as their characters.

- **Option 3:** Find a safe place in your community where students can line up, in costume and in character, and encourage passers-by to ask their questions. This can be fun if you have a small town center, shopping area, or other safe, accessible area where people gather. In this case, be sure to have students practice ahead of time.

Biography Role-Play *(cont.)*

Differentiation Strategies

- **Above grade level**—Have these students pick a person outside this lesson—this way you will have a full class of unique characters and it will be more fun for guests to interact with your class (instead of asking and hearing answers to the same questions from the same characters). This also allows the lesson to be more open-ended, which challenges these students to be creative.

- **Below grade level**—Instead of having students memorize answers to this lesson's questions, allow them to write answers on the backs of the relevant note cards. Ask students to practice these answers until they can read them fluently. If you like, decrease the overall number of questions for which students are responsible.

- **English language learners**—Work with these students to create questions and answers for each biography (instead of having them do this independently). Once you have listed on your classroom board at least five questions and answers for each biography, allow students to choose the person they will role-play and to pick three of the listed questions/answers to memorize.

Assessment

1. During the activity, walk through the room giving each student a score from 1-10 based on effort and participation.

2. While students are answering questions in character, you ask the questions. Grade students using the following guide.

    1 = does not meet expectations
    2 = meets expectations
    3 = exceeds expectations

    - The student had the correct amount of questions on note cards.

    - The student knew the answers to the questions.

    - The student performed effectively as the character.

3. Collect students' note cards and assess them using the *Traits of Good Writing* (page 22) or the assessment strategy of your choice.

TIME Magazine Biographies

TIME Magazine Biographies Table of Contents

Madeleine Albright

MAY 17, 1999 $3.50

TIME

THE REVIEW IS IN!

At Ramstein Air Base
in Germany, talking to the
Ukrainian Foreign Minister
last Wednesday

Albright at War

**EXCLUSIVE: Behind the scenes with the Secretary of State
as she pushes for victory in Kosovo**

Madeleine Albright

She helped redefine America's role in the world.

May 17, 1999

"What's at stake here is the principle that aggression doesn't pay, that ethnic cleansing cannot be permitted." The troops gathered at an air base in Germany to cheer. Secretary of State Madeleine Albright is explaining the war in Kosovo to them. It is, to her, a defining mission for America. For someone who had to flee Hitler and Stalin as a child, it is also a very personal mission. As President Clinton said when she was finished, "Secretary Albright, thank you for being able to redeem the lessons of your life story by standing up for the freedom of the people in the Balkans."

"Just because you can't act everywhere doesn't mean you don't act anywhere."

The Kosovo conflict is often referred to as Madeleine's War. More than anyone else, Albright represents the vision of America's role in the world that brought the United States into this war. To Albright, a peaceful Europe is central to U.S. interests. Upholding human rights and opposing ethnic cleansing are central to our values. Because of what she learned as a child, she believes that America's interests cannot be easily separated from its values.

For Albright, standing aside in the face of terrible acts committed by the Serbs in Kosovo was not an option. Her greatest success so far has been to create and then maintain unity among the 19 NATO nations supporting the Kosovo war. Every morning she gets up at 6:00 to begin her daily round of hand-holding phone calls around the world. The goal is simple: make sure that no country wavers from NATO's aims or sends mixed signals to Serbian President Slobodan Milosevic.

Do interventions like the one in Kosovo represent a new view of America's role in the world after the Cold War? How do we pick and choose such fights? Why Kosovo and not Rwanda? "There is not a simple formula. I happen to believe, and argued so at the time, we should have done more in Rwanda. We get involved where the crime is huge, where it's in a region that affects our stability, and where there is an organization capable of dealing with it. Just because you can't act everywhere doesn't mean you don't act anywhere. We're evolving these rules."

Madeleine's War? "Well, I don't think it's solely mine. But I feel that we did the right thing, and I am proud of the role I played in it." Now her challenge is to show that she is as good at getting out of a war as she is at getting into one.

Madeleine Albright

Key Dates

1937 — Born in Czechoslovakia on May 15

1948 — Immigrates with her family to Colorado

1976 — Receives advanced degree in International Affairs from Columbia University

1978–1981 — Works as staff member on National Security Council

1993–1996 — Serves as U.S. delegate to the United Nations

1997 — Becomes the first female secretary of state and the highest-ranking woman in the President Bill Clinton administration

Focus: Reading for Understanding

1. What was the war in Kosovo about? Why is it referred to as "Madeleine's War"? Examine the cover image.

2. Why did Madeleine Albright—both personally and as an American official—believe the United States should enter the war in Kosovo?

3. What was Albright's strategy against President Slobodan Milosevic?

4. What is Albright's explanation of how the United States decides which conflicts to get into?

5. Word Watch—Look up the following words and note how they are used in the article: *aggression, ethnic cleansing, permitted, defining, redeem, upholding, opposing, wavers, interventions, stability,* and *evolving*.

Connect

"Just because you can't act everywhere doesn't mean you don't act anywhere." Do you agree or disagree with this statement? Write about a time this was true for you. Or, explain why you disagree.

Explore

1. What role does the secretary of state play? Write a job description.

2. Where is Kosovo? Where is Rwanda? Learn more about the wars of ethnic cleansing in both places.

3. What is NATO? Find out why and how it was formed and which countries are members.

4. Where did Albright grow up? Learn more about her past.

Corazon Aquino

JANUARY 5, 1987 $1.95

TIME

WOMAN OF THE YEAR

Philippine President Corazon Aquino

Corazon Aquino

A housewife who moved her people with softness

January 5, 1987

For her determination and courage in leading a democratic revolution that captured the world's imagination, Corazon Aquino is TIME's "Woman of the Year" for 1986.

Whatever else happens in her rule as president of the Philipines, Aquino has already given her country a bright and inviolate memory. More important, she has also revived its sense of identity and pride. In the Philippines, those luxuries are especially precious. Almost alone among the countries of Asia, it has never been steadied by an ancient culture; its sense of itself, and its potential, were further worn away by nearly four centuries of Spanish and American colonialism.

But Aquino's revolution with a human face—the democratic defeat of dictator Ferdinand Marcos—was no less a triumph for women the world over. The person known as the "Mother of the Nation" managed to lead a revolt and rule a republic without ever giving up her calm or her gift for making politics and humanity companionable.

Inevitably, the fairy-tale nature of Aquino's sudden rise prompted myths. To some, the woman seemed a Joan of Arc, a reflection of her people's hope as she led them to freedom. To others, she was a Cinderella. Yet, the real world does not lend itself to fable for long. The day after her victory, Aquino found herself in charge of one of the world's most desperate countries. Her country was saddled with a foreign debt of $27 billion. It had 20,000 armed Communist guerillas and a pile of government institutions that bore Marcos's corrupt mark.

It was not just her softness that impressed, but the unexpected toughness that underwrote it.

Admittedly, Aquino has stumbled due to her innocence and inexperience. But when challenges arose, the political newcomer rose to meet them.

At year's end, Aquino's problems have not diminished. Yet her authority seemed as steady as her gift for confounding expectations. To come to power, Aquino had only to be herself, a symbol of sincerity and honesty. But to stay in power, she had to transcend herself. After ten months in office, it was not just her softness that impressed, but the unexpected toughness that underwrote it. It was not just her idealism, but a steely pragmatism that made it more rigorous. It was not just her rhyme, but her reason. Aquino moved people, in both senses of the word, by making serenity strong and strength serene.

Corazon Aquino

Key Dates

1933 — Born in Tarlac, Philippines

1946 — Moves with her family to the United States

1953 — Returns to the Philippines

1955 — Marries young politician Benigno Aquino

1983 — Husband assassinated during his campaign

1986 — Defeats Ferdinand Marcos to become the first woman president of the Philippines

1987 — New constitution for the Philippines is ratified in February

1992 — Returns to being a private citizen

2000 — Heads foundation to spread democracy throughout Asia

Focus: Reading for Understanding

1. Corazon Aquino's husband was campaigning for president of the Philippines. What happened to him?

2. What did Aquino restore to the Philippines?

3. After 10 months in office, what did people respect about Aquino?

4. Word Watch—Look up the following words and note how they are used in the article: *pragmatism*, *steely*, *rigorous*, *serenity*, *idealism*, *guerillas*, *Communist*, and *dictator*.

Connect

1. Aquino beat Ferdinand Marcos to become the first woman president of the Philippines. Geraldine Ferraro was the first woman to be nominated as vice president of the United States. What do these two women have in common? What are their differences?

2. What experiences and qualities do you think a woman needs to lead a nation? Do you know women who have these qualities?

Explore

1. What is Communism? Research the Communist theology. Are there any Communist countries today? Name them.

2. Aquino became head of a foundation to help spread democracy throughout Asia. What is the name of this foundation? Has it been successful?

Louis Armstrong

Louis Armstrong
To him jazz was like telling a story.

February 21, 1949

Jazz trumpeter Daniel Louis Armstrong and New Orleans jazz grew up together. Armstrong says: "Jazz and I grew up side by side when we were poor." The wonder is that both jazz and Armstrong emerged from streets of brutal poverty: jazz to become an exciting art, Armstrong to be hailed almost without dissent as its greatest creator/practitioner.

In his boyhood New Orleans, jazz was simply a story told in strongly rhythmic song. It was pumped out "from the heart" with a nervous, exciting beat. To trumpeter Armstrong, jazz is still storytelling: "I like to tell people things that come naturally."

From the place Armstrong and jazz were born, there was no direction to move but up. Armstrong came up from what was then the toughest section of New Orleans. His parents were the nearly illiterate grandchildren of slaves. Nearby were Fisk School where he learned to read and write and music halls where both the music and the dancing were brassy. At night, the rhythm came at him from every direction. In the daytime, the music came from musicians playing in the streets.

At first, Armstrong just listened to the music and learned how to read it. But then, he picked up musical instruments—first the tambourine and drums, then the bugle and cornet. Finally, Armstrong settled on the trumpet. Armstrong's fame spread while spending two years playing on riverboats up and down the Mississippi River. "He wasn't much to look at on the riverboat. Just a little guy with a big mouth. But, man, how he could blow that horn!" recalls one fan.

Today, Armstrong tours the United States, Canada, and Europe with his band. He appears in movies and makes best-selling records.

> **…both jazz and Louis emerged from streets of brutal poverty: jazz to become an exciting art, Armstrong to be hailed almost without dissent as its greatest creator/ practitioner.**

Happy-go-lucky Armstrong will never be in financial need. Should he have to lay down his gleaming horn tomorrow, he would collect $864 a month for life. But Armstrong is still mighty fit and expects to keep fit for a long time. How long does he think he can last? "Right until I get to the Pearly Gates, I hope. " When he gets to those gates he is going to pay his respects, he says, to another famous trumpeter. Says Armstrong: "I'm gonna blow a kiss to Gabriel."

Louis Armstrong

Key Dates

1900 — Born on July 4 in New Orleans, Louisiana

1919 — Leaves New Orleans for the first time to play in St. Louis

1922 — Joins King Oliver's Creole Jazz Band in Chicago

1932–1935 — Tours and lives in Europe; Meets the King of England

1956 — Plays trumpet and sings in musical High Society; Tours Africa

1964 — His recording of "Hello, Dolly!" reaches #1

1971 — Dies in New York City on July 6

Focus: Reading for Understanding

1. What does Louis Armstrong say about jazz? How does Armstrong plan on paying his respects to the Angel Gabriel?

2. What are the different types of instruments that Armstrong played before settling on the trumpet?

3. At the beginning, Armstrong spent two years playing on riverboats up and down which river?

4. Word Watch—Look up the following words and note how they are used in the article: *dissent, hailed, trumpeter, brutal, illiterate, brassy, bugle,* and *cornet.*

Connect

Find out about Marian Anderson. How are her experiences with music similar or different from those of Armstrong?

Explore

1. The article states that jazz could only move in an upward direction. Research the history of jazz music. Make a list of other prominent jazz musicians.

2. At the time of this article in 1949, it stated that Armstrong would collect $864 a month for life. What type of money do famous musicians make today?

Neil Armstrong

Neil Armstrong

He was the first man to walk on the moon.

July 25, 1969

The ghostly, white-clad figure slowly descended the ladder. Having reached the bottom rung, he lowered himself into the bowl-shaped footpad of Eagle, the spindly lunar module of *Apollo 11*. Then, he extended his left foot, cautiously, tentatively, as if testing water in a pool and was, in fact, testing a wholly new environment for man. That groping foot, encased in a heavy multi-layered boot (size 9 1/2B), would remain indelible in the minds of millions who watched it on TV, and a symbol of man's determination to step—and forever keep stepping—toward the unknown.

"That's one small step for [a] man; one giant leap for mankind."

After a few short but interminable seconds, U.S. astronaut Neil Armstrong placed his foot firmly on the fine-grained surface of the moon. The time was 10:56 P.M. (EDT), July 20, 1969. Pausing briefly, the first man on the moon spoke the first words on lunar soil: "That's one small step for man, one giant leap for mankind."

With a cautious, almost shuffling gait, the astronaut began moving about in the harsh light of the lunar morning. "The surface is fine and powdery; it adheres in fine layers, like powdered charcoal, to the soles and sides of my foot," he said. "I can see the footprints of my boots and the treads on the fine, sandy particles."

Minutes later, Armstrong was joined by Edwin ("Buzz") Aldrin. Then, gaining confidence with every step, the two jumped and loped across the barren landscape for 2 hours and 14 minutes, while the TV camera they had set up some 50 feet from Eagle transmitted their movements with remarkable clarity to enthralled audiences on Earth, a quarter of a million miles away. Sometimes moving in dreamlike slow motion, sometimes bounding around in the weak lunar gravity like exuberant kangaroos, they set up experiments and scooped up rocks, snapped pictures and probed the soil, apparently enjoying every moment of their stay in the moon's alien environment.

After centuries of dreams and prophecies, the moment had come. For the first time, man had set foot on another world. Standing on the lifeless, rock-studded surface, Armstrong could see Earth, a lovely blue-and-white hemisphere suspended in the velvety black sky. The spectacular view might well help him place his problems, as well as his world, in a new perspective.

The astronauts' feat was far more than an American triumph. It was a shining reminder that whatever man imagines, he can bring to pass.

Neil Armstrong

Key Dates

1930 — Born in Wapakoneta, Ohio, on August 5

1962 — Enters astronaut training program

1969 — Serves as commander of the *Apollo 11* lunar mission and is the first person to set foot on the moon

1971 — Becomes professor of aerospace engineering at the University of Cincinnati

1985 — Appointed by President Ronald Reagan to the National Commission on Space

Focus: Reading for Understanding

1. Examine the cover. Why is Neil Armstrong carrying an American flag? Why does he need the spacesuit he is wearing and the gear he is carrying?

2. What were Armstrong's first words on the moon? What does this line mean?

3. Word Watch—Look up the following words and note how they are used in the article: *clad, spindly, tentatively, groping, indelible, interminable, gait, adheres, loped, bounding, barren, transmitted, enthralled, exuberant, prophecies, perspective,* and *feat.*

Connect

1. What would you have said if you were the first person to reach the moon? Brainstorm ideas in class and share them out loud or in writing.

2. Have a class debate about whether U.S. tax dollars should be spent on space exploration. Divide into two teams and, before the debate begins, come up with lists of pros and cons in order to anticipate the other side's arguments.

Explore

1. Until the mid-1900s, the idea of man walking on the moon seemed like a fantasy. What do you predict will be possible in the future? Discuss as a class, and then write a short piece of fiction about your idea. Or, write a newspaper article from the future in which you report on the development you predicted.

2. Who is John Glenn?

Menachem Begin and Anwar Sadat

Menachem Begin and Anwar Sadat

They gave peace a chance in the Middle East.

September 25, 1978

From the beginning it had been one of the most remarkable meetings of world leaders ever. In the end it turned out, against all expectations, to be a summit of astonishing historic achievement. After 13 days of being cloistered with their closest aides at Camp David, President Jimmy Carter, Egyptian President Anwar Sadat and Israeli Premier Menachem Begin emerged Monday night to sign two documents that were giant efforts toward peace in the Middle East.

Though considerable obstacles remain, it was a major breakthrough in areas that have defied all the efforts of war and diplomacy for three decades. The outcome was more than anyone except perhaps host Jimmy Carter had believed possible before the summit began and more than had been anticipated right up to the Sunday on which the summit was to end, apparently in failure.

The size of their triumph was evident as the three leaders spoke in turn Sunday night at the White House. Carter announced the broad outlines of the two agreements, declaring, "My hope is that the promise of this moment will be fulfilled." Sadat praised Carter for calling the summit. "You took a giant step," he said.

Begin, chatty at first, turned serious to sound the same note of praise. "Peace now celebrates a great victory for the nations of Egypt and Israel and for all mankind." Turning to Sadat, Begin recounted how they had become friends on first meeting, when Sadat made his historic visit to Jerusalem last November.

"Peace now celebrates a great victory for the nations of Egypt and Israel and for all mankind."

Never in the history of modern international negotiations have leaders been so isolated for so long in an attempt to resolve the differences that have divided their nations. In contrast to the deadly serious items on the negotiating table, was the lovely setting of Camp David, with an enchanting hint of autumn in the air. Also unusual was the meeting's nearly total isolation from the probes of the world's press. It may well have been the strict secrecy that enabled the conference to go on as long as it did and thus make possible Sunday's dramatic turnabout.

Seldom has such an extraordinary trio of leaders gathered in common purpose: a Christian, a Jew and a Muslim, each a man of deep faith who believes that while he is responsible for the welfare of his people, he also serves a higher authority. This can humble a leader; but it can also encourage him to take worthwhile or dangerous risks. And despite all the dangers that lie ahead, there can be no dispute about one point: the summit moved the troubled Middle East a little closer to peace and a little farther from war.

Menachem Begin and Anwar Sadat

Key Dates

1913 — Begin is born in Poland on August 16.

1918 — Sadat is born in Egypt on December 25.

1970 — Sadat is elected president of Egypt.

1977 — Begin is elected prime minister of Israel.

1978 — Begin and Sadat win Nobel Peace Prize for their roles in the Camp David Peace Accords.

1981 — Sadat is assassinated October 6.

1992 — Begin dies of natural causes.

Focus: Reading for Understanding

1. What was the purpose of the meeting involving Anwar Sadat, Menachem Begin, and Jimmy Carter? Why was the United States part of this summit? What were the results?

2. How did being isolated at Camp David (a presidential retreat in Maryland) without reporters help the peace negotiations?

3. "He also serves a higher authority." What does the author mean in describing each leader this way?

4. Word Watch—Look up the following words and note how they are used in the article: *summit, cloistered, aides, obstacles, diplomacy, anticipated, negotiations, isolated, turnabout, welfare, humble,* and *dispute.*

Connect

1. What links do you see to Golda Meir?

2. Is there an issue in your school that could be constructively addressed through a summit? Come up with a proposal that describes what you would do.

Explore

What is happening in the Middle East today? How has the peace process been advanced or hindered by recent events?

Queen Elizabeth Bowes-Lyon

TIME

THE WEEKLY NEWSMAGAZINE

QUEEN ELIZABETH
"Let your light so shine before men. . . ."
(Foreign News)

Queen Elizabeth Bowes-Lyon

She represents Britain's women and earned their love.

October 9, 1939

At 11:35 A.M. September 3, 1939, the first air-raid warning sounded over London. Some eight-million unhurried Londoners tramped down the steps of their air-raid shelters, among them King George VI and Queen Elizabeth. Half an hour later, the all-clear signal given, George and Elizabeth emerged. For him, the war had begun. For her, as for some 15 million other British women, the prewar life of home and children and firesides and friends had stopped.

Better than ever before, Britain's Queen represents British womanhood. She was already a typical British wife. She had her own visiting, inspecting, and encouraging jobs to do. On a 24-hour schedule, she simply went where she thought she ought to go. And, when she had time, she went to visit her two daughters who, like so many other English children, were sent out of London to avoid German bombs. No British queen had ever spent a month more like the month spent by her subjects, and the parallel example had not been lost on the Empire.

Her Majesty is the first Scotswoman in over eight centuries to marry an English king. Two days after her marriage to the Duke of York (who became King George VI), Elizabeth was made a royal princess. She asked her friends to keep on calling her Lizzie.

"She is one of us!" became what everyone said of Elizabeth, "the smiling duchess." When once asked what she would say if her husband unexpectedly became king and she the queen, Elizabeth quietly replied: "I don't know what I would say. I only hope it would be something which would prove to the English people how much I love them."

"She is one of us!" became what everyone said of Elizabeth.

Every act of King George VI and Queen Elizabeth since their coronation has proved that they understand what is expected of them by the British Empire. In peacetime Elizabeth once said, "If we make up our minds to try and solve our problems in good friendship and out of love for one another and for our country, we will somehow and sometime, I think, get things set right."

Queen Elizabeth Bowes-Lyon

Key Dates

1900 — Born on August 4 in England

1923 — Marries Prince Albert at Westminster Abbey on April 26

1926 — Their first child, Princess Elizabeth, is born

1937 — Prince Albert is crowned King George VI

1939 — Britain and Germany go to war (World War II begins)

1952 — King George dies and daughter Princess Elizabeth becomes Queen Elizabeth II; Elizabeth becomes Queen Mother

2000 — Celebrates her 100th birthday on August 4

2002 — Dies on March 30

Focus: Reading for Understanding

1. Why were King George and Queen Elizabeth climbing down into an air-raid shelter?

2. Queen Elizabeth was originally from which country?

3. What name did friends call Queen Elizabeth? What did the people of England call her?

4. Word Watch—Look up the following words and note how they are used in the article: *majesty, firesides, coronation, Empire, emerged, air raid, tramped, shelters,* and *typical.*

Connect

1. What challenges did Queen Elizabeth have from being an "outsider" of England? Have you ever felt like an "outsider?" What challenges did you have to overcome? Share these with the class.

2. Queen Elizabeth's actions showed her love and concern for others. What were some of the things that she said or did to show her concern?

Explore

1. Research the English monarchy. How far back can you trace it? Make a list of as many kings and queens of England as you can. Compare your list with the lists of other students in the class.

2. Learn more about Queen Elizabeth II, the daughter of Queen Elizabeth. What are her responsibilities in Great Britain?

George H. W. Bush

George H. W. Bush
A president tested by war

January 7, 1991

"George Bush seemed almost to be two presidents in 1990," observed TIME's editors. They praised Bush for his strong role in shaping foreign policy. But they added that his handling of domestic affairs was marked by confusion and wavering. The editors went on to make an unusual decision: instead of selecting a single "Man of the Year", they named "the two George Bushes" as 1990's "Men of the Year." Two images of Bush appeared on the magazine's cover to illustrate this point.

He asked a simple question: "What happens if we do nothing?"

During the days after his inauguration, George Bush delighted in leading guests on private tours of the White House. He often paused in front of a favorite painting showing Abraham Lincoln with his generals during the Civil War. "He was tested by fire," Bush would say, "and showed his greatness." And to one friend, Bush wondered aloud how he might be tested, whether he too might be one of the handful of presidents destined to change the course of history. On August 1 he found out.

It was about 8 P.M. when an aide informed Bush that Iraq had invaded Kuwait. At first, it appeared that Saddam Hussein would only attack as far as the long-disputed border. But then Iraqi tanks churned into the Kuwaiti capital, forcing the royal family to flee. It was a full-blown takeover. There was little sense that big U.S. interests were at stake until the president spoke. He asked a simple question: "What happens if we do nothing?"

This was the moment for which he had spent a lifetime preparing. And Bush's instincts were only confirmed as it became clear what would happen if Iraq were allowed to swallow Kuwait. If Iraq succeeded, tyrants around the world would learn that aggression pays.

Against the judgment of many advisers, Bush was convinced that Saddam must be stopped now, before he became even more dangerous. Bush decided that he, not Saddam, would shape the new world order taking shape after the end of the Cold War. He wanted to see the United States and the Soviet Union work together through the United Nations to reach the goal of security for all promised by the U.N.'s founders in 1945. Bush thus found the "vision," at least in foreign policy, that he has long lacked.

Bush's answer to the question he posed at the beginning of the crisis—"What happens if we do nothing?"—was not to sit back and watch how events played out, as he had done so often before. It was to move, quickly and skillfully, to confront an act of aggression that might have set a dangerous example for the world. His next moves could determine what future presidents say when they gaze at his portrait on the White House wall.

George H. W. Bush

Key Dates

1924 — Born in Milton, Massachusetts, on June 12

1940–1945 — Serves as youngest Navy pilot in World War II

1966–1970 — Serves as representative from Texas in Congress

1971–1973 — Serves as ambassador to the United Nations

1974–1975 — Chief of the U.S. Liaison Office in People's Republic of China

1976–1977 — Director of Central Intelligence Agency (CIA)

1980–1988 — Vice president of the United States under President Ronald Reagan

1988–1992 — 41st president of the United States

Focus: Reading for Understanding

1. Examine the cover. Why are there two photos of President George Bush? What aspects of Bush does each photo portray?

2. What happened on August 1, 1990? How and why did Bush make the decision to lead the United States into the Gulf War?

3. What lessons did Bush think the world would learn if Saddam Hussein were allowed to act with no consequences? What message did Bush send by committing U.S. troops?

4. Word Watch—Look up the following words and note how they are used in the article: *inauguration, destined, invaded, long-disputed, churned, full-blown, confirmed, aggression, tyrants, Cold War,* and *lacked.*

Connect

Draw a portrait of yourself. Model it on the drawing of Bush on this cover. Which two parts of yourself have you represented? Write a headline to go with your picture.

Explore

Locate Iraq and Kuwait on a world map. Why did Iraq invade Kuwait? Find out more about Saddam Hussein and the Gulf War.

George W. Bush

George W. Bush

Finally president after the wildest election in U.S. history

December 25, 2000

For a proud son of a one-term president, could there be a more humbling path to power than this? You could almost see the weight of it when Bush rose last Wednesday night with tears in his eyes and promised, "I will work to earn your respect," all but admitting it does not just come with the job when you win this way.

"I'm a results-oriented person."

George W. Bush campaigned for a year against partisan politics. He staged the most inclusive Republican Convention in memory, surrounded himself at every chance with poor schoolchildren whom he promised he would not leave behind. In the end he won a smaller percentage of the African American vote than any Republican since Barry Goldwater. The comics joked that he won 100% of the black vote where it mattered most—on the Supreme Court. But Bush himself admits that the greatest misconception about him is that he is not racially sensitive. He can point to Colin Powell and Condoleezza Rice, but it won't change the fact that 40% of the African Americans who went to the polls in Florida were new voters, and many wonder if their votes were even counted.

If the task ahead seems impossible given how the race ended, it is worth remembering how it began. Bush came to the field with less experience in public life than just about anyone in a century. He confronted a sitting vice president with the wind at his back and maintained a nearly unbroken lead for more than a year, even though more people agreed with the other guy's positions. Stripped of every winning Republican issue—the cold war, crime, the economy—he proceeded to run on Democratic ones: education, health care, Social Security. But he ran a more disciplined race than we have seen in years and made his inexperience a virtue and his vagueness a shield.

That was enough to keep him in the race far longer than the computer models projected, if not enough to win him the most votes. But then came the "second campaign." The way he played told us more about him than anything he had said as a candidate. Through the five-week Florida recount, he stood back and stayed out of the fray. He hired the best people, gave them their freedom, and held them accountable.

So, the first election of the new millennium is finally over. The cast has scattered and the chads have been swept away. All through the campaign, George W. Bush practiced for the moment when he would put his hand in the air and swear to uphold the Constitution and the honor and dignity of the office. But while the office has at last been won, the honor remains to be earned.

George W. Bush

Key Dates

1946 — Born on July 6 in New Haven, Connecticut

1968 — Graduates from Yale

1968–1973 — Flew as an F–102 fighter pilot in the Texas Air National Guard

1975 — Earns Master's degree in business administration from Harvard

1988 — Senior advisor to his father's presidential campaign

1994 — Elected governor of Texas, defeating Ann Richards in her reelection bid

1998 — Reelected as governor of Texas

2000 — Elected president of the United States

2004 — Reelected president

Focus: Reading for Understanding

1. Why did George W. Bush have to earn respect as president of the United States?

2. What were the issues on which Bush campaigned?

3. According to the profile, how did Bush handle himself during the Florida recount?

4. After reading the article, describe Bush. What are his strengths and weaknesses?

5. Word Watch—Look up the following words and note how they are used in the article: *humbling, partisan, inclusive, misconception, virtue, vagueness, chads,* and *millennium.*

Connect

1. What impressions do you have of Bush's legitimacy as president of the United States?

2. How do you think most people feel about the 2000 election?

3. Would you have voted for Bush? Why or why not?

Explore

1. What is the Electoral College? Research how a president of the United States is elected.

2. How are Presidents George W. Bush and George H. W. Bush similar? How are they different?

Jimmy Carter

Jimmy Carter

An outsider who defied expectations

January 3, 1977

Just a year ago, he was walking up to men and women who did not know he existed, shaking their hands and drawling, "I'm Jimmy Carter, and I'm going to be your next president." The notion seemed preposterous. Most political professionals were sure he did not have a chance—but none of the voters laughed in his face. He was such an engaging man—a trifle shy, despite all his boldness. There was that sunburst of a smile that people would always remember. Right from the start, he was seen as being a rather different kind of politician compared with the rest of the field. He not only knew what he wanted; he also sensed, at least in the primary elections, what the American people wanted.

The result was something of a political miracle.

On January 20, he will place his left palm on the Bible and raise his right hand. Then, in the now familiar soft and even tones of South Georgia, Jimmy Carter, 52, will take the oath that will make him the 39th president of the United States.

When Carter was walking the icy streets of New Hampshire last January, as many as 40% of the local people did not even know who he was. He occupied no political office. His one term as Georgia's governor had expired in January 1975, and state law kept him from running again. He was the typical outsider. It was widely assumed that outsiders—particularly those from the South—went nowhere nationally.

But all the assumptions were demolished by Carter's will power, his almost arrogant self-confidence, his instinct to ask his listeners to "Trust me," and his promise to give them "a government as good and as competent and as compassionate as are the American people." The talk about trust and love sounded vague to many. But he was a candidate of the 1970s, and he knew that the voters were more concerned about the issue of moral leadership than about continuing the big-spending liberal programs of the 1960s.

Most political professionals were sure he did not have a chance—but none of the voters laughed in his face.

Carter did more than just defeat a dozen other Democrats, most of them senators and governors who were better known and had bigger power bases. By showing that a non-racist Southerner could win a major party nomination, Carter gave new pride to his region and went far to heal ancient wounds.

In the end, Carter won by 51% to Gerald Ford's 48%. Because of his impressive rise to power, because of the new phase he marks in American life, and because of the great anticipations that surround him, James Earl Carter Jr. is TIME's "Man of the Year."

Jimmy Carter

Key Dates

1924 — Born in Plains, Georgia, on October 1

1962 — Wins election to the Georgia Senate

1971 — Becomes governor of Georgia

1976–1980 — President of the United States

1982 — Founds the Carter Center in Atlanta

1991 — Launches the Atlanta Project, a communitywide effort to attack the social problems associated with poverty

2002 — Awarded Nobel Peace Laureate

Focus: Reading for Understanding

1. How was Jimmy Carter viewed at the beginning of his campaign? Why was his success seen as a "political miracle"?

2. How is Carter portrayed in this article? On the cover?

3. Why were the American people particularly concerned with moral leadership in the 1970s?

4. Why was Carter selected as TIME's "Man of the Year" for 1976?

5. Word Watch—Look up the following words and note how they are used in the article: *defied, drawling, preposterous, trifle, oath, expired, assumed, demolished,* and *arrogant.*

Connect

1. Would you have voted for "the peanut farmer from Georgia" for president? Why or why not?

2. Both Bill Clinton and Carter were Democrats. What are the similarities and differences in these Democratic presidents?

Explore

What were the highlights of Carter's campaign and term as president? What has he gone on to do since leaving office?

Fidel Castro

Fidel Castro

He led a revolution in Cuba.

January 26, 1959

The executioner's rifle cracked across Cuba last week, and around the world voices cheering for a new democracy fell still. The men who had just won a popular revolution for old ideals—for democracy, justice and honest government—themselves picked up tools of dictatorship. As its public urged them on, the Cuban rebel army shot more than 200 men, hastily convicted in battlefield courts, as torturers and mass murderers for the fallen Batista dictatorship. The constitution, which outlaws the death penalty, was ignored.

The only man who could have silenced the firing squads was Fidel Castro Ruz, the 32-year-old lawyer, fighter and visionary who led the rebellion. And Castro was in no mood for mercy. "They are criminals," he said. "Everybody knows that. We give them a fair trial. Mothers come in and say, 'This man killed my son.'"

No Cuban voices rose in protest, though there were doubtless many private misgivings. Overwhelming public opinion, especially among women, urged the firing squads on.

As he walked with his entourage through the lobby of the Havana Hilton last week, Castro stopped to talk with two old women who blubbered a request that their murdered sons be remembered. "It is because of people like you," said Castro, hugging the pair, "that I am determined to show no mercy."

Castro has confidence, physical courage, shrewdness, generosity, and luck. He won his long war not by fighting but by perching in self-confidence on the highest mountain range in Cuba for more than two years. He became the symbol of his rebellious country. He pulled quarreling rebel factions together and inspired them to face down a modern army.

"I am determined to show no mercy."

By 1958, Castro's force had grown to some 2,000 guerrillas. Financial support and weapons came from landowners and businessmen opposed to the corrupt Batista regime. Toward the end of 1958, Castro's rebels took over the city of Santa Clara, a city of 150,000. Then, on New Year's Day 1959, Batista fled into exile, and his army surrendered. Rebel commanders sped into Havana and took over the key military posts.

For the next week Fidel Castro received the ovation of his islanders in a triumphal march to the capital. Even before he reached Havana, the record shops were selling a new song:

> Fidel has arrived,
> Fidel has arrived,
> Now we Cubans are freed
> From the claws of the tyrant.

Fidel Castro

Key Dates

1927 — Born on May 13

1950 — Earns Ph.D. in law from University of Havana

1953–1955 — Captured and imprisoned

1956 — Leads armed attacks against Batista's government

1959 — Forces Batista into exile

1959–1976 — Prime minister of Cuba

1961 — The United States severs diplomatic relations with Cuba

1976 — Becomes Cuba's head of state, president of Council of State, and president of Council of Ministers

Focus: Reading for Understanding

1. What happened in Cuba when Fidel Castro's army overthrew Batista?

2. "We give them a fair trial," said Castro of the men he and his brother ordered executed. What was really going on?

3. What does the Havana Hilton story reveal about Castro?

4. How did Castro rise to power? Who were his supporters? What happened to Batista?

5. What is ironic about the song Cubans sang in 1959?

6. Word Watch—Look up the following words and note how they are used in the article: *dictator, executioner, firing squad, misgivings, entourage, blubbered, shrewdness, perching, factions, guerrilla, corrupt, regime, exile,* and *ovation.*

Connect

Find references to Cuba and Castro in the news today.

Explore

1. In 1961, the United States cut off diplomatic relations with Cuba. Why?

2. Find out what happened in the 2000 Elian Gonzales case.

3. Look at the cover. What happened on July 26 (the date on the flag)? Hint: The year in question is 1953.

Carrie Chapman Catt

FIFTEEN CENTS

TIME

The Weekly News-Magazine

AN IOWA FARMER'S DAUGHTER
Mrs. Carrie Chapman Catt
(See Page 8)

Vol. VII, No. 24   June 14, 1926

Carrie Chapman Catt

A farmer's daughter fights for women's rights.

June 14, 1926

In Paris this week, women's rights groups from around the world met at the International Woman Suffrage Alliance. The opening of the conference was enlivened by a purely American brawl. The National League of Women Voters represents the United States in the alliance. The National Women's Party was on hand asking admission as a second U.S. organization.

Though the two groups both support women's rights, they can't agree on how women should be guaranteed these rights. The league wants special legislation protecting working women. The party opposes protection and wants absolute equality for women and men.

The admissions committee votes against the National Women's Party because one important woman—Mrs. Carrie Chapman Catt, founder of the alliance—said no. "After women won the vote in the United States," said Mrs. Chapman, "the Women's Party worked for a federal amendment to give equal rights under the law for women and men." Such an amendment, Catt felt, would either take away from women the protection they fought for or bring men under the same laws. "The women workers have no organizations (such as unions) as men do," Mrs. Chapman pointed out. "They need protection."

Born on a farm, Catt worked her way through Grinnel College in just three years. At age twenty-two, she was superintendent of schools in Mason City, Iowa. She married struggling country editor Leo Chapman at age twenty-five. A widow at thirty, she sold advertisements for a San Francisco newspaper. In San Francisco, she met and married George Catt, and most of her work for women's rights started then.

She is the most likely named woman who could be president.

In 1900, she succeeded Susan B. Anthony as president of the American Woman Suffrage Association. Catt labored tirelessly for the Nineteenth Amendment to the U.S. Constitution—guaranteeing a woman's right to vote—until its adoption in 1920. Composed, forceful, direct, Catt has faced many stormy situations. And though now retired at age sixty seven, her name is still a word to reckon with in women's circles.

In recent years, women's groups and the powerful women who lead them have multiplied. But, one must credit Mrs. Catt with having gone the furthest as a leader of women's rights. Despite her advancing age, she is most likely to be named when an old-time suffragist is asked: "What woman could be president of the United States?"

Carrie Chapman Catt

Key Dates

1859 — Born January 9 in Ripon, Wisconsin

1886 — Becomes San Francisco's first female newspaper reporter

1890 — Works with Susan B. Anthony to reorganize the National American Woman Suffrage Association (NAWSA)

1892 — Addresses Congress on the proposed suffrage amendment

1900 — Succeeds Anthony as the NAWSA president

1902 — Organizes the International Woman Suffrage Alliance

1920 — The Nineteenth Amendment giving women the right to vote is passed

1945 — Dies on March 9 in New Rochelle, New York

Focus: Reading for Understanding

1. What were the two groups that worked in support of women's rights at the International Suffrage Alliance?

2. What are some adjectives that could be used to describe Carrie Chapman Catt and her involvement with women's rights?

3. Who did Catt succeed as president of the American Woman's Suffrage Association?

4. Word Watch—Look up the following words and note how they are used in the article: *suffrage, enlivened, brawl, amendment, alliance, legislation, reckon, unions,* and *opposes.*

Connect

1. What are some of Catt's life experiences that helped her become a leader of the women's movement?

2. Compare and contrast Carrie Chapman Catt's experiences as a leader of a specific group to those of Eva Perón and Corazon Aquino. Discuss these differences and similarities.

Explore

1. Research the women's movement in the United States over the past 100 years. Make a time line of key events.

2. Who are some of the leaders of the women's movement today? What are the issues for women today?

Cesar Chavez

JULY 4, 1969

TIME

THE GRAPES OF WRATH, 1969
MEXICAN-AMERICANS ON THE MARCH

CESAR CHAVEZ

112

Cesar Chavez

He fought to improve conditions for farm workers.

July 4, 1969

ITEM: At a fashionable New Hampshire prep school, grapes are the only part of the meal left untouched.

ITEM: In San Francisco, an official of Safeway Supermarket observes: "We have customers who come to the store for no other reason than to buy grapes. They'll load up their car with grapes and nothing else."

ITEM: In Oakland, a conscience-ridden housewife explains apologetically: "I really wanted to have this dessert, and I just decided that one little bunch of grapes wouldn't make that much difference."

La huelga (the grape strike) is symbolic of Mexican Americans' quest for a full role in U.S. society.

Why all the excitement about this smooth, sweet and innocent fruit? The answer is that the table grape, *Vitis vinifera*, has become the symbol of the four-year-old strike of California's predominantly Mexican American farm workers. For more than a year now, table grapes have been the object of a national boycott that has won the sympathy and support of many Americans—and the intense anger of many others.

Field work remains one of the most unpleasant of human occupations: it demands long hours of backbreaking labor, often in choking dust amid insects and under a flaming sun. Workers frequently live in shacks without light or plumbing.

The strike, known as *la causa*, represents not only a protest against working conditions among California grape pickers but the wider aspirations of the nation's Mexican American minority as well. *La causa*'s magnetic champion and the country's most prominent Mexican American leader is Cesar Estrada Chavez, 42. *La causa* is Chavez's whole life. For it, he has impoverished himself and endangered his health by fasting. He urges his people—nearly five million of them in the United States—to rescue themselves from society's cellar. As he sees it, the first step is to win the battle of the grapes.

While *la huelga* (the grape strike) is in some respects a limited battle, it is also symbolic of the Mexican American's quest for a full role in U.S. society. What happens to Chavez's farm workers will be an omen, for good or ill, of the Mexican American's future. For the short term, Chavez's aspiration is to win the fight with the grape growers. If he can succeed in that difficult and uncertain battle, he will doubtless try to expand the movement beyond the vineyards and into the entire Mexican American community.

Cesar Chavez

Key Dates

1927 — Born near Yuma, Arizona, on March 31

1962 — Elected president of National Farm Workers Association

1968 — Calls for nationwide boycott of all California grapes

1988 — Fasts for 36 days to call attention to the link between pesticides in grapes and cancer in children of farm workers

1993 — Dies on April 23

1994 — Posthumously awarded the Presidential Medal of Freedom

Focus: Reading for Understanding

1. What is a boycott? A strike? What reactions do the three opening scenarios illustrate?

2. What was *la causa*? What was its goal and who was its leader?

3. Explain in your own words the idea that Cesar Chavez wanted to rescue Mexican Americans from "society's cellar." According to this comparison, who would be in "society's attic"?

4. Word Watch—Look up these words and note how they are used in the article: *predominantly, boycott, sympathy, protest, magnetic, prominent, omen, aspiration,* and *posthumously.*

Connect

1. Have you witnessed or ever taken part in a strike, boycott, or other protest? What issues were involved? Was the protest successful?

2. What would you have done during *la huelga*? Write a letter to a friend explaining your position.

Explore

1. Find out more about Chavez's life and the results of the grape strike.

2. What other leaders do you know about who fought for minority rights?

3. To what does the cover line "The Grapes of Wrath, 1969" refer?

Winston Churchill

TWENTY CENTS

HALF-CENTURY SUPPLEMENT
★★★ WITH 4 PAGES OF COLOR MAPS ★★★

TIME

THE WEEKLY NEWSMAGAZINE

MAN OF THE HALF-CENTURY
He launched the lifeboats.

$6.00 A YEAR

Winston Churchill

A statesman who inspired the free world

January 2, 1950

He was a kingly figure. He was his nation's savior, Britain's greatest statesman, the leader and inspiration of the free world. Yet Winston Churchill was an intensely human hero. He was easily moved to rage or tears. He delighted in mischief and rushed headlong into many an action he was later to regret.

Churchill was born and raised amid the splendors of Blenheim Palace, the 320-room mansion that a grateful nation gave to his ancestor, John Churchill, for his victory over the French in the Battle of Blenheim in 1704. His mother was a beautiful American heiress, Jennie Jerome; his father the brilliant but unsteady politician Lord Randolph Churchill.

> ## "I have nothing to offer but blood, toil, tears, and sweat."

School bored young Winston. He was a poor student who most loved playing with his enormous collection of toy soldiers. Fame and glory were always his motivation.

During the dismal era when Adolf Hitler was rising and Britain shuttered its windows to the world, Churchill urged his fellow members of the House of Commons to take action. Thanks to a wide network of information gatherers, Churchill's knowledge of Hitler's ambitions was extensive. Churchill spoke out bitterly against the inaction of Britain's Prime Minister Neville Chamberlain, arguing that Hitler was a bully who would only respond to force.

When Britain finally declared war against Germany in 1939, the government at last turned to Churchill. In the spring of 1940, as Hitler invaded the Low Countries and the tide turned toward Britain, Chamberlain was turned out. With Hitler preparing to pounce, Churchill took the reins as prime minister with the ringing declaration, "I have nothing to offer but blood, toil, tears, and sweat."

Single handedly, Churchill rallied his people to resist Hitler. No detail was too small to escape his attention. He never tired of inspecting troops or chatting with victims of the blitz. He often had to be dragged protesting from a rooftop as London shuddered under a German attack.

Some of the passages of Churchill's wartime speeches are as stirring today as anything in Shakespeare. For example, Churchill vowed that Britain would fight "to the end" in a 1940 speech to the House of Commons:

"We shall go on to the end. We shall fight in France, we shall fight in the seas and oceans . . . we shall defend our island, whatever the cost may be. We shall fight on the beaches. We shall fight on the landing grounds, we shall fight in the fields and in the streets, we shall fight in the hills; we shall never surrender."

And fight they did. That a free world survived in 1950, with a hope of more progress and less calamity, was due in large measure to the efforts of Winston Churchill.

Winston Churchill

Key Dates

1874 — Born in Oxfordshire, England, on November 30

1901 — Enters House of Commons

1911–1915, 1939–1940 — Serves as First Lord of the Admiralty

1940–1945, 1951–1955 — Prime minister of Great Britain

1953 — Knighted; wins Nobel Prize for literature

1955 — Resigns as prime minister

1964 — Retires from House of Commons

1965 — Dies in London

Focus: Reading for Understanding

1. Describe Winston Churchill's educational and family background.

2. How did Churchill stand up to Hitler in World War II?

3. When did Churchill become prime minister? What did he mean when he said he had nothing to offer "but blood, toil, tears, and sweat"?

4. Read the excerpt from the 1940 speech aloud. How are Churchill's speeches described?

5. Word Watch—Look up the following words and note how they are used in the article: *statesman, inspiration, headlong, heiress, motivation, dismal, shuttered, network, ambitions, extensive, inaction, invaded, single-handedly, rallied, resist, blitz, shuddered, passages, stirring, vowed,* and *calamity*.

Connect

How are Adolf Hitler, Joseph Stalin, and Margaret Thatcher associated with Churchill?

Explore

1. Look up some of Churchill's speeches and analyze their style. What makes them so powerful?

2. For what did Churchill win the Nobel Prize in literature?

Bill Clinton

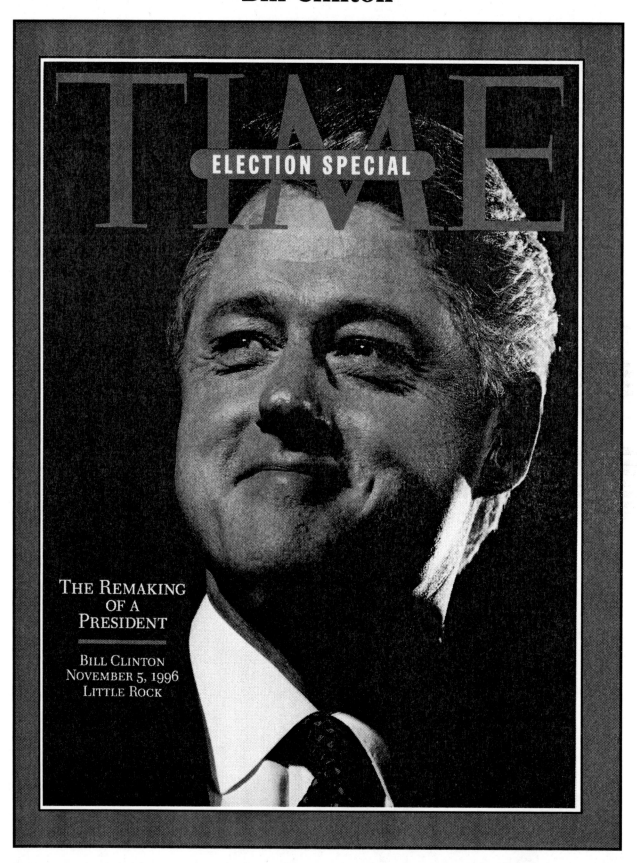

ELECTION SPECIAL

THE REMAKING
OF A
PRESIDENT

BILL CLINTON
NOVEMBER 5, 1996
LITTLE ROCK

Bill Clinton

The first two-term Democrat since FDR

November 18, 1996

A nation born of a distrust of kings won't easily forgive a president who behaves too much like one. And so every four years, the people give a test: first we hand someone the most powerful job in the world. Then, we demand that he not be too proud of himself for having it or too sure that he alone knows what to do with it. And then we sit back and watch, until it's time to decide whether to reelect him.

In four years, Bill Clinton learned that it is not enough to be smart or charming or full of vision. His win on Tuesday night was a triumph. But to win, Clinton had to swallow his pride. He had to embrace his enemies and borrow their ideas. He offered small proposals, not great visions. He will march into history as the first two-term Democrat since Franklin Roosevelt not with great leaps forward but one baby step at a time.

"It is time to put politics aside, join together and get the job done for America's future," Clinton said on the steps of the old statehouse in Little Rock on Tuesday night. Four years ago, in that same place, the night was a party, dressed in windbreakers and jeans and set to rock tunes. This year, it was a serious speech in a blue suit on a red carpet with background music by the composer Aaron Copland: "'Tis a gift to be simple, 'tis a gift to be free."

What was historical about Tuesday was not that a Democratic president was reelected for the first time since 1936 or a Republican Congress for the first time since 1930.

It was that in 220 years, no Democrat has been elected to the White House when the Congress was controlled by the opposition. We have never been here before.

To win reelection, Clinton had to embrace his enemies and borrow their ideas.

And we did not get here by accident. After a campaign in which the two parties together spent more than half a billion dollars getting their messages out, the voters finally had their chance to send one back: We have too little faith in either party to let one of you govern unchecked. And we have too many problems that have to be solved to trust either of you to do it alone.

Having campaigned in 1992 to make grand changes—only to fail to make them as president—Clinton ran in 1996 pledging to fix problems bit by bit—and won. By promising less, he gained back the trust of a majority of voters. He passed the test. As a result, the first Democrat in two generations to win a second term may actually have earned the chance to make some history.

Bill Clinton

Key Dates

1946 — Born in Hope, Arkansas, on August 19

1968–1970 — Rhodes Scholar at Oxford University in England

1973 — Obtains law degree

1975 — Marries Hillary Rodham

1978–1980, 1982–1992 — Serves as governor of Arkansas

1992 — Elected as 42nd president of the United States

1996 — Reelected president

1999 — Following an extensive investigation and a 21-day impeachment trial, Clinton is acquitted by the Senate on charges of perjury and obstructing justice.

2004 — Published his autobiography, *My Life*

Focus: Reading for Understanding

1. Explain the first sentence of the article. How is America a "nation born of distrust of kings"? Hint: Think about the American Revolution.

2. What was historic about Bill Clinton's election to a second term?

3. According to the writer, what message did voters send to their political parties in the 1996 election?

4. How did Clinton's campaign change from 1992 to 1996? Why did he take this new approach?

5. Word Watch—Look up the following words and note how they are used in the article: *distrust, proposals, opposition, campaigned, pledging, majority,* and *generations.*

Connect

1. What impressions do you have of Clinton's presidency? What highs and lows do you recall? How do you think he will be remembered?

2. Hillary Rodham Clinton was a nontraditional First Lady. What has she done since the Clintons left the White House?

Explore

1. Who was vice president under Bill Clinton? What was he known for, and what is he doing today?

2. Should presidents be allowed to serve more than two terms? How many terms did Franklin Roosevelt serve? What made it possible for him to be reelected president more than once?

Hillary Rodham Clinton

EVEREST: THE MOVIE
STOCKS: WHY '97 ISN'T '87

Turning Fifty

**Hillary Clinton, confronting
a birthday and a newly empty
nest, embodies the challenge
facing Baby Boom women:
What's the next act?**

Hillary Rodham Clinton
A First Lady determined to make an impact

October 20, 1997

In September 1995, relations between the United States and China were tense. Some in Washington urged First Lady Hillary Rodham Clinton to cancel her trip to Beijing, where she planned to speak at the United Nations' Fourth World Conference on Women. But the First Lady went anyway. When she reached the speaker's podium, Clinton unleashed the most stinging human-rights attack ever by a prominent American representing this government on Chinese soil. "It is time to break our silence," she declared. "It is time for us to say here in Beijing, and the world to hear, that it is no longer acceptable to discuss women's rights as separate from human rights."

Without mentioning China by name, the First Lady offered a long list of abuses there and elsewhere, including denial of political rights and suppression of speech. The address lost bits here and there in translation as it made its way to the headphones of women from more than 180 countries. But if at times her words took a moment or two to register, Clinton's message got through clearly enough. Delegates cheered, others leaped from their seats and pounded the tables. The applause lasted more than 20 minutes after she left the stage. Women she has met since in Soweto, Budapest, and Manila can recite the lines she delivered that day.

The freedom she feels abroad may explain why Clinton spends so much time there. She is by far the United State's most traveled First Lady. In Bangladesh, an entire village was named for her. But those trips did little to help her come to terms with her skeptical audience at home. That was why, on the plane back from Beijing, in Ireland and in Latin America, the computer-illiterate First Lady curled up with a legal pad on her lap to write *It Takes a Village*. The book, the First Lady's observations on American children, took almost a year to complete.

> ## "It is no longer acceptable to discuss women's rights as separate from human rights."

As her critics might have expected, she wrote glowingly of expensive social programs, such as France's child-care system. But, the book also provided glimpses of a surprisingly conservative side. She advocated school uniforms. She praised the "heartening efforts" of Promise Keepers to strengthen marriage.

Unlike her most recent predecessors, who were nearer retirement age when they left the White House, Clinton's chance to make a mark did not end when the helicopter rose from the South Lawn for the last time. "I'll go on to do something else that I find challenging and interesting," she promised.

Hillary Rodham Clinton

Key Dates

1946 — Born in Chicago, Illinois, on October 26

1975 — Marries Bill Clinton who she met at Yale Law School

1977 — Founds Arkansas Advocates for Children and Families

1980 — Daughter Chelsea is born

1992 — Becomes First Lady

1993 — Heads Task Force on National Health Care Reform

1996 — *It Takes a Village* is published

2000 — Elected to U.S. Senate seat from New York

2008 — Runs to gain the Democratic presidential nomination

Focus: Reading for Understanding

1. What message did First Lady Hillary Clinton offer at the UN's conference on women in Beijing? Why did she criticize China? How did women around the world react to Clinton's speech?

2. How did Clinton decide to write *It Takes a Village*? What is it about? Why was it important to her?

3. Word Watch—Look up the following words and note how they are used in the article: *urged, podium, unleashed, stinging, human rights, prominent, suppressed, address, register, skeptical, illiterate, critics, advocated,* and *predecessors.*

Connect

1. Clinton feels that women's rights cannot be separated from human rights. Do you agree?

2. Compare Clinton to Eleanor Roosevelt. Is Clinton the kind of First Lady that Eleanor Roosevelt was? What similarities and differences do you see?

Explore

What is Clinton doing now? What happened during her 2008 campaign for president? What do you think she'll be remembered for as First Lady?

Margaret Chase Smith and Lucia Cormier

Margaret Chase Smith and Lucia Cormier

Two women who want to be called senator

September 5, 1960

On a summer's day in 1848, a hoop-skirted housewife stood up in Wesleyan Chapel in Seneca Falls, New York, and read the eighth of eleven resolutions to the delegates at the first U.S. women's rights convention. Elizabeth Cady Stanton read: "It is the duty of the women of the country to secure for themselves the sacred right of the elective franchise." The delegates were aghast at such a daring notion. "Why Lizzie," cried Lucretia Mott, "thee will make us ridiculous!"

Together, they are the symbols and the harvesters of the long, bittersweet struggle for women's rights.

In the summer of 1960, a century after Stanton's declaration and 40 years after the Nineteenth Amendment guaranteed the right to vote regardless of sex, the emancipated women of the United States are far from ridiculous. They form the largest single element in the American electorate (56.1 million women of voting age versus 52.7 million eligible men). Next November 8 will likely go down in history as Ladies' Day with women voters outnumbering men for the first time in any peacetime presidential election.

In addition, three women are running for the U.S. Senate, 26 women for the House of Representatives, and more than 100 women for legislatures and other statewide offices. The nation's biggest, most eye-catching feminine contest is building up in Maine, where two women are matched, for the first time ever, in a race for the U.S. Senate.

The two candidates offer the Down East voters a remarkable choice. As the senior senator from Maine, Margaret Chase Smith, 62, is a cool, silver-haired, sometimes tart-tongued Republican who has won the esteem of her colleagues and the nation with her diligence, independence, and courage.

Her opponent, Lucia Marie Cormier, 48, is an ex-schoolteacher and the proprietress of a Rumford, Maine, gift shop, a Roman Catholic of French Canadian descent, effective minority leader of the state legislature and the darling of Maine's resurgent Democrats.

Separately, the ladies from Maine will fight their political battles without catcalls. Together, they are the symbols and the harvesters of the long, bittersweet struggle for women's rights.

No matter which of the ladies wins the election, women permeate U.S. politics so thoroughly as to indicate that they have only begun to fight. As voters, party workers, and politicians, they will play a larger, more important role in the affairs of state in the 1960s and their voices will be heard, emphatically, through the likes of Margaret Chase Smith and Lucia Cormier.

Margaret Chase Smith and Lucia Cormier

Key Dates

1916 — Jeanette Rankin becomes first woman elected to national office (U.S. House of Representatives)

1920 — The Nineteenth Amendment giving women the right to vote is passed

1925 — Nellie Tayloe Ross becomes first female governor (Wyoming)

1932 — Hattie Caraway becomes first woman elected to U.S. Senate

1933 — Francis Perkins becomes first woman cabinet member (Secretary of Labor)

1984 — Geraldine Ferraro becomes first woman vice presidential candidate of a major party

Focus: Reading for Understanding

1. What were Margaret Chase Smith and Lucia Cormier running for in the summer of 1960? From which state were they running?

2. Why was November 8, 1960, called "Ladies' Day"?

3. What experience did Smith and Cormier bring to this position?

4. Word Watch—Look up the following words and note how they are used in the article: *senator, colleagues, emancipated, harvesters, emphatically, catcalls,* and *element.*

Connect

1. How did Carrie Chapman Catt's accomplishments affect the lives of Smith and Cormier?

2. Get personally involved with politics! Write a letter to your U.S. senator informing him or her on a current political issue you support.

Explore

1. Research information on Elizabeth Cady Stanton. Who was she? How did she change the freedom and opportunities for women?

2. Research to find out how many of the U.S. senators today are female. Who are they?

Eve Curie

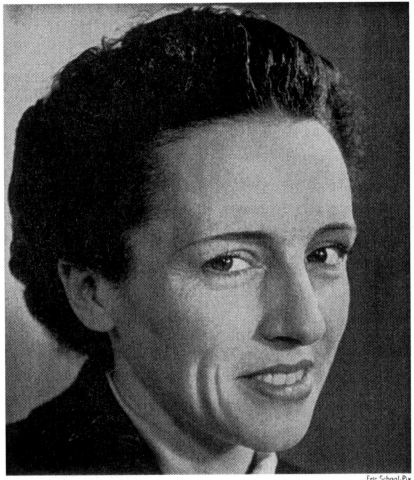

TIME

THE WEEKLY NEWSMAGAZINE

Eric Schaal-Pix

EVE CURIE

"All the men and women of genius are with us."
(Foreign News)

Eve Curie

The official spokesperson for all French women in World War II

February 12, 1940

Last week, Eve Curie visited Mrs. Franklin Delano Roosevelt at the White House in Washington, D.C. From there, Curie would start her two-month lecture tour of the United States to discuss French women and the war.

Five million Frenchmen are now in uniform. Although Germany has some six million men under arms, the Reich is almost twice as populous as France and does not have the same manpower shortage that France has on the home front. Thus, there has been no question for millions of French women of not seeking war work. French women are working at three kinds of jobs: (1) in agriculture; (2) in industry, chiefly armaments; and (3) in the social services.

To White House correspondents, Miss Curie emphasized the point that French women are out to bring the war to a decisive finish. "Peace will not come soon," she said, "and it will not come at all while the Hitler regime remains in Germany because the French are determined that when this war ends there will be no more fighting in Europe for a long time."

The Nobel Prize has gone three times to the Curies—once to Mother Marie and her husband Pierre, the late great discoverers of radium, once to Mother Marie alone, once to Marie's daughter Irene, the co-discoverer of synthetic radioactivity. But never to elegant daughter Eve, whose brilliant biography *Madame Curie* was a bestseller all over the United States.

"Peace will not come soon and it will not come at all while the Hitler regime remains in Germany."

As a young woman, Curie took to music and living an unconventional life. She became a concert pianist and escaped into a Paris that her scientist family will never know. "I don't hate science; it just terrifies me!" says Curie. Miss Curie started writing music criticism for various papers under a pen name. From this, she drifted into adapting Broadway plays for the Paris stage.

Curie's mother was Marie Curie. She died in 1934. Publishers in the United States asked Curie to write a biography of her mother. Curie was willing and after being constantly jogged by her publishers, turned out a smooth, satisfying, and deeply moving work.

Eve Curie

Key Dates

1904 — Born December 6 in Paris, France

1937 — Publishes bestselling book *Madame Curie*

1940 — Moves to England and works for the Allied and Free French causes during World War II

1952 — Appointed special advisor to the secretary general of NATO

1954 — Marries Henry R. Labouisse

1954 — Works with UNICEF; visits more than 100 developing countries seeking to help children

1958 — Becomes a U.S. citizen

2007 — Dies in New York at age 102

Focus: Reading for Understanding

1. What did Eve Curie come to Washington to discuss?

2. Who are some of the other famous Curies mentioned in the article? For what are they famous?

3. How did Curie feel about science?

4. Word Watch—Look up the following words and note how they are used in the article: *regime, pen name, radium, jogged, populous, unconventional, decisive, manpower,* and *successor.*

Connect

1. The biography *Madame Curie*, written by Eve Curie, was a bestseller all over the United States. Read a book review of this book. What do the reviews say of this book written and published in the 1930s?

2. Write a biography of an individual you admire.

Explore

1. Curie went on a lecture tour to discuss the French women and their role in the war. What role did women in France and the United States play during World War II?

2. Curie later worked with UNICEF. What is this organization, and what are its goals?

Walt Disney

TIME

The Weekly Newsmagazine

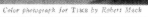

Color photograph for TIME by Robert Mack

Volume XXX

HAPPY, GRUMPY, BASHFUL, SNEEZY, SLEEPY, DOC, DOPEY, DISNEY
The boss is no more a cartoonist than Whistler.
(See CINEMA)

Number 26

Walt Disney

He created the world's most popular mouse.

December 27, 1937

Even artists say that Walter Elias Disney is an artist. Some go further and say that he is a great one. Certainly his works are better known and more widely appreciated than those of any other artist in history.

> ## Disney's works are better known than those of any other artist in history.

But Disney the artist is nowhere near as widely known as his legendary creation, Mickey Mouse—or any of Mickey's cartoon companions. In fact, when some art historian of the future sets out to trace the rise of the animated cartoon, the quest for original drawings by Disney will be about as difficult as it is to locate authentic paintings by Rembrandt. Walt Disney has not drawn his own pictures for nine years. To turn out the mass production issued nowadays under his name, he would have to have 650 hands. And 650 hands he has. His cinema factory produces an average of 12 Mickey Mouse films every year. Were Disney to undertake the involved processes of drawing, coloring, and photographing the 15,000 sketches that go into one of these shorts, the feat would approach Michelangelo's job on the Vatican ceiling.

Released this week was the latest Disney venture, *Snow White and the Seven Dwarfs*, the most ambitious animated cartoon ever attempted. It took Disney's many hands over three years to make.

Some in Hollywood had wondered whether a fairy story could have enough suspense to hold an audience through seven reels, and whether an audience would care about the fate of characters who were just drawings. But Disney has done it again. *Snow White and the Seven Dwarfs* is as exciting as a Western, as funny as a comedy. It is a masterpiece, to be shown in theaters and beloved by new generations for years to come.

The strangest sights in the Disney plant are found in the animation department. There, animators peer into mirrors, leap up and down, squawk, and then sketch the effects. Years ago, there was a "zoo" at the Disney studios, and animators would study the animals in preparing their scenes. But for some years, it has been recognized that the best cartoon effects are not to be gotten from animals acting like animals, but from animals acting like people. Mickey Mouse always looked like a human from the start. He has the large, soft eyes and pointed face of his creator. And Mickey's voice? It is the voice of Walt Disney himself.

Walt Disney

Key Dates

1901 — Born in Chicago on December 5

1923 — Opens cartoon studio in Hollywood

1928 — Launches Mickey Mouse, an instant sensation, in the first talking cartoon

1932 — Wins first of a record 32 personal Oscars

1937 — Premieres *Snow White*, first full-length animated film

1955 — Opens Disneyland

1964 — Conceives Epcot Center, built in Orlando, Florida

1966 — Dies in Los Angeles

Focus: Reading for Understanding

1. "Even artists say that Walter Elias Disney is an artist," notes the writer. Trace this idea throughout the article. What examples does the author use to support this point?

2. How did Disney produce his cartoons? Describe the "strange sights" that were found in Disney's animation department.

3. What were critics' concerns about *Snow White* before the movie was released? What did TIME's writer think of the actual film? Look at the cover.

4. Word Watch—Look up the following words and note how they are used in the article: *animated, quest, authentic, mass production, undertake, feat, ambitious, venture, fate, masterpiece, generations,* and *squawk.*

Connect

1. Watch Disney's *Snow White and the Seven Dwarfs* and write your own review of it.

2. Have you seen any other Disney cartoons? Which is your favorite? Why?

3. Do you agree that Disney is an artist?

Explore

1. Find out more about how animated cartoons are made. Draw one frame of a cartoon you would like to make and write a summary of the plot for your cartoon.

2. Research the lives and work of Rembrandt and Michelangelo, the artists Disney is compared to in this article.

3. Learn more about the history of animation from early Disney cartoons to computer animation by pioneers like John Lasseter (the creator of *Toy Story*).

Thomas Edison

FIFTEEN CENTS

TIME

The Weekly News-Magazine

THOMAS ALVA EDISON
Ich dien
(See Page 16)

VOL. V., No. 21

MAY 25, 1925

Thomas Edison

His invention reshaped the modern world.

May 25, 1925

Thomas Edison first appeared on TIME's cover in 1925. The article below was written for a special 1999 issue on the most influential people of the millennium.

"Genius," Thomas Alva Edison once remarked, "is about 2% inspiration and 98% perspiration." Or again, as he said in his autobiography, "There is no substitute for hard work." Edison's tireless work habits took shape during his childhood in Port Huron, Michigan. His formal education, according to most accounts, lasted only three months. His mother, herself a former teacher, educated him for a while at home, but the boy's growing fascination with chemistry soon led him into a rigorous course of independent study. To pay for the materials needed for his experiments, Edison, at age 12, got a job as a candy and newspaper salesman on the Grand Trunk Railway. By the time he was 16, he had learned telegraphy and began working as a telegraph operator at various points in the Middle West; in 1868, he joined the Boston office of Western Union. It was here that he decided to work full time as an inventor.

His first patent, for an electric vote recorder, taught him a lesson that would guide the rest of his career. There was no demand, at the time, for electric vote recorders, and his device earned him nothing. Edison vowed never again to invent something unless he could be sure it was commercially marketable.

In 1876, he created the world's first industrial-research facility in Menlo Park, New Jersey. Some think that Menlo Park itself was Edison's most influential invention.

"There is no substitute for hard work."

Edison—known as the Wizard of Menlo Park—is commonly called the inventor of the light bulb. In truth, he and his coworkers accomplished far more than that. In 1879, they created an incandescent lamp with a carbonized filament that would burn for 40 hours, but a working laboratory model was only the first step. How could they make this device illuminate the world? For this they would need a host of devices, including generators, motors, junction boxes, safety fuses, and underground conductors, many of which did not exist. Amazingly, only three years later, Edison opened the first commercial electric station on Pearl Street in lower Manhattan. It served roughly 85 customers with 400 lamps and pioneered the process of turning night into day.

Edison amassed more than 1,000 patents, including one for the movie camera. He never lost the relentless desire to learn and to make things that had intrigued him as a boy. Once, he was signing a guest book and came to the "interested in" column. Edison wrote, "Everything."

Thomas Edison

Key Dates

1847 — Born in Milan, Ohio, on February 11

1868 — Receives his first patent (of a total of 1,093) for the Electrographic Vote-Recorder

1876 — Opens Menlo Park research facility

1877 — Invents the carbon-telephone transmitter for the Western Union Telegraph Company

1878 — Patents the first phonograph

1879 — Creates incandescent lamp

1931 — Dies at age 84

Focus: Reading for Understanding

1. For which invention is Thomas Edison most famous? What else did he invent?

2. What did Edison decide after his electric vote recorder failed to make any money?

3. Explain Edison's definition of *genius*. Do you agree with his observation?

4. Word Watch—Look up the following words and note how they are used in this article: *inspiration, perspiration, rigorous, patent, commercially, industrial, incandescent, filament, host, device, supervisor, amassed,* and *relentless.*

Connect

1. Edison claimed to be interested in "everything" as a boy. Make a list of all the things you are interested in and share them in class.

2. Brainstorm a list of ideas for inventions. Choose one and describe it as if you were applying for a patent. What will your invention do? How would you make it? Sketch it.

Explore

1. Learn more about how a light bulb works.

2. What is a patent? Apart from those listed here, what were some of Edison's 1,093 patents for?

Albert Einstein

Albert Einstein

His name is a synonym for genius.

December 31, 1999

On December 31, 1999, TIME selected Albert Einstein as the Person of the Century, declaring that he had done more than any other individual to influence the preceding 100 years. Runners-up for this distinction were Mohandas Gandhi and Franklin Roosevelt.

As the twentieth century's greatest thinker, Einstein best embodies what historians will remember about the past 100 years.

In a century that will be remembered foremost for its science and technology—in particular for our ability to understand and then harness the forces of the atom and the universe—one person stands out as both the greatest mind and symbol of our age: the kindly, absentminded professor whose wild hair, piercing eyes, and extraordinary brilliance made his face a symbol and his name a synonym for genius: Albert Einstein.

During his spare time as a young officer in a Swiss patent office in 1905, Einstein produced three papers that changed science forever. The first, for which he was later to win the Nobel Prize, described how light could behave not only like a wave but also like a stream of particles, called quanta or photons. This insight provided the foundation for such twentieth-century advances as television, lasers, and semiconductors.

Einstein went on to show that energy and matter were merely different faces of the same thing, their relationship described by the most famous equation in all of physics: energy equals mass multiplied by the speed of light squared, $E=mc^2$. Although not exactly a recipe for an atomic bomb, it explained why one was possible. He also helped resolve smaller mysteries, such as why the sky is blue. (It has to do with how molecules of air diffuse sunlight.)

His crowning glory, perhaps the most beautiful theory in all of science, was the general theory of relativity, published in 1916. It was based on a thought experiment: imagine being in an enclosed lab accelerating through space. The effects you'd feel would be no different from the experience of gravity. Gravity, he figured, is a warping of space-time. The general theory opened up an understanding of the largest of all things, from the Big Bang of the universe to its mysterious black holes.

As the century's greatest thinker, as an immigrant who fled from oppression to freedom, Einstein best embodies what historians will regard as significant about the twentieth century. And as a philosopher with faith both in science and in the beauty of God's handiwork, he personifies the legacy that has been bequeathed to the next century.

Albert Einstein

Key Dates

1879 — Born in Ulm, Germany, on March 14

1902 — Works at Swiss patent office

1905 — Publishes three papers on theoretical physics

1916 — Proposes general theory of relativity

1922 — Wins Nobel Prize in Physics

1933 — Emigrates to Princeton, New Jersey

1939 — Urges FDR to develop atom bomb

1955 — Dies in his sleep on April 18

Focus: Reading for Understanding

1. Why was Albert Einstein chosen as TIME's "Person of the Century?" Which of his scientific discoveries or theories are highlighted in this article?

2. Why does the author feel that Einstein "best embodies what historians will remember about the twentieth century"?

3. Word Watch—Look up the following words and note how they are used in the article: *foremost, patent, particles, insight, foundation, advances, merely, diffuse, accelerating, warping, subatomic, oppression, embodies, handiwork, personifies, legacy,* and *bequeathed.*

Connect

Brainstorm a list of people you would nominate for Person of the Century. Write a profile of your favorite.

Explore

What is the Nobel Prize? Who else has won it in physics? What practical applications (such as television) have these winners been responsible for?

Dwight Eisenhower

Dwight Eisenhower

He brought prosperity to the nation.

July 4, 1955

In the 29 months since Dwight Eisenhower moved into the White House, a remarkable change has come over the nation. The blood pressure and temperature have gone down; nerve endings have healed over. The new tone could be described in a word: confidence.

The United States is moving forward. New homes, new factories and new office buildings are being built in and around the cities. Small businesses—ranging from clothing shops to hamburger stands—are springing up. In labor union meetings, most of the talk now centers on how to get new benefits, not on how to keep up with a runaway cost of living. And at office coffee breaks, the talk has become easy and calm, not about the coming war or the coming depression. These days, moderation is the rule.

A large part of the new U.S. mood is the enormous confidence of the American people in the president. Eisenhower's popularity was shown last week as he toured through Vermont, New Hampshire, and Maine, meeting the people and being plied with gifts of chickens, trees, boots, a red knit cap, a chainsaw, and a tablet of granite.

Even more significant than the people's confidence in the president is the president's confidence in the people. Eisenhower does not believe that the people have to be whipped up to do what is necessary to oppose the march of Communism. Eisenhower does not believe that the people have to be directed into prosperity.

When Ike was a candidate for president, Democratic challengers recalled the pain of the Great Depression and asked whether a Republican president—particularly one who had little experience in civilian life and would have to depend on Republican financial advisers—would bring on another depression.

Even more significant than the people's confidence in the president is the president's confidence in the people.

Within weeks after he took office, the new president began to apply to a prosperous but jittery United States the basic philosophy of free enterprise. He wiped out most remaining government controls, set tax policies to encourage investment and expansion in business and industry, and applied, where possible, the policy of letting the marketplace set the pace of the economy. Federal spending was cut, and along with it, taxes lowered.

After this considerable shift in economic policy, the United States is more prosperous than ever before. The nation is now producing more goods and services than it ever did. Personal income is higher than ever. And the market value of shares on the New York Stock Exchange has increased $61 billion since January 1953.

Dwight Eisenhower

Key Dates

1890 — Born in Denison, Texas, on October 14

1915 — Graduates from West Point

1942 — Becomes commander of U.S. forces in Europe during World War II

1950 — Serves as supreme commander of the forces of the North Atlantic Treaty Organization (NATO)

1952–1960 — Serves as U.S. president

1957 — Sends federal troops to uphold school desegregation in Little Rock, Arkansas

1969 — Dies on March 28

Focus: Reading for Understanding

1. What caused the new U.S. mood?

2. What did Dwight Eisenhower's visit to New England reveal about how people felt about him?

3. When Eisenhower was campaigning, what did people fear? How did he calm these fears after he was elected?

4. What signs of U.S. prosperity does the article mention? What was Eisenhower's idea of the role of the federal government?

5. Word Watch—Look up the following words and note how they are used in the article: *springing, runaway, cost of living, depression, moderation, plied, prosperity, candidate, civilian, jittery, philosophy, free enterprise, Federal, considerable, shift, income,* and *market value.*

Connect

1. How do you feel about the current president?

2. Does the current president inspire the same kind of confidence Eisenhower did? Why or why not?

Explore

1. Find out more about Eisenhower's life before he became president.

2. Why do you think the Liberty Bell was chosen to illustrate this cover?

Geraldine Ferraro

Geraldine Ferraro
A path-breaking candidate for vice president

July 23, 1984

The audience is clapping. Vice President Walter Mondale appears surprised. He acknowledges the woman standing to his right, as if seeing her for the first time. He smiles, she smiles back. The applause grows loud. "Let me say that again," says the delighted Mondale. "This is an exciting choice!" The crowd goes wild. Mondale is clapping too. Does he know yet what he has done?

Does anyone know what happened midday last Thursday in the Minnesota statehouse? If this were Great Britain or India, whose pulse would race? But here? It couldn't happen here. The professionals think they can explain it. As Walter Mondale's running mate in the 1984 presidential election, Geraldine Ferraro doesn't balance the Democratic ticket philosophically, being liberal, pro-union and all. But the gender gap is the key to everything: more women, more votes. Got it. But wasn't something else involved in Mondale's decision to propose a woman for vice president of the United States? Or did we only imagine that the nation whooped, quaked, froze, and beamed?

And it wasn't only the women-ought-to-be-locked-in-the-kitchen nation or the women-are-better-than-God nation, either. It was the great, quiet, don't-bother-me middle, awakened by a stroke to a new set of feelings and fumbling to put them in order.

History. So this is how it's made. One tends to think of history making in terms of treaties and crownings, but it's the mind that makes the changes. Come November, a woman from Tulsa (or Hartford or Butte) will hear the curtain of the voting booth shut behind her, and she will be alone with America and her own life. Another woman's name will be on the ballot before her. No matter how she votes, her thoughts about her place in the world will not be the same again.

The world's most powerful nation may be ready to be led by a woman.

In the long run, what happened in Minnesota was not just politics. The selection of Ferraro will affect not only the woman in the voting booth. It will be equally felt by the man who—today, next month, next year—stares across his desk or dining room table and sees someone as if for the first time.

There is no history to lean on, nothing Americans can do now but work the matter out for themselves and see where the re-jiggled republic stands. The world's most powerful nation may be ready to be led by a woman, and any woman at all may prepare herself to lead it. This is an exciting choice.

Geraldine Ferraro

Key Dates

1935 — Born in Newburgh, New York, on August 26

1960 — Earns law degree

1979–1985 — Elected to three terms in the U.S. House of Representatives

1984 — Becomes the first woman nominated for the vice presidency by a major political party

1984 — Democrats Walter Mondale and Ferraro are defeated in general election by Republicans Ronald Reagan and George Bush

1992 — Runs for U.S. Senate and loses by a narrow margin

Focus: Reading for Understanding

1. At what point in the article does the reader find out what is going on? What is the effect of writing the story this way?

2. Why would a female political candidate not be surprising in Great Britain or India? (See the profile of Margaret Thatcher in this collection.)

3. How does the author predict Mondale's choice will affect women? Men?

4. Word Watch—Look up the following words and note how they are used in the article: *gender, propose, whooped, quaked, beamed, treaties, crownings, re-jiggled,* and *republic.*

Connect

Do you think America is ready for a female president? Explain your answer.

Explore

1. Women did not have the right to vote until the Nineteenth Amendment was added to the Constitution in 1920. Research the contributions of suffragettes Carrie Chapman Catt, Susan B. Anthony, and Elizabeth Cady Stanton.

2. Are there many female political leaders where you live? In your state legislature? Representatives to Congress from your state? Find out from the League of Women Voters chapter in your area.

Gerald Ford

Gerald Ford

He helped heal the nation after Watergate.

August 19, 1974

Two hours earlier, the East Room had been the setting for Richard Nixon's farewell speech to his Cabinet and the White House staff. Pictures of Nixon and scenes from his triumphant Peking and Moscow visits had disappeared from the corridor leading to the Oval Office. They were replaced by pictures of Gerald (Jerry) Ford and his family. Now the East Room was filled again with 250 guests, a few of them still red-eyed from weeping at the emotional Nixon farewell.

"You have not elected me as your president by your ballots."

The stage was set for the transfer of the world's most powerful political office from Richard Nixon to Gerald Ford. Shortly after noon, everyone in the East Room rose as a military aide announced: "Ladies and gentlemen, the Chief Justice of the United States." Warren Burger strode into the room to administer the oath of office. Although his role was traditional, Burger's presence had special meaning. As Chief Justice of the Supreme Court, he was symbolic of the law and of the constitutional processes that, set in motion by the excesses of the president and the men around him, had inevitably led to Nixon's toppling.

As Burger entered, the vice president and Mrs. Ford were announced. They walked, amid thunderous applause, into the same stately chandeliered room Richard Nixon and his family had left a short while before.

The exit and entrance were powerful reminders of the smoothness with which the American system can transfer the world's most powerful office from one man to another. Ford raised his right hand, placing his left on a Bible held by his wife, Betty. Then, at 12:03 P.M., repeating the oath of office, Gerald Ford formally became the 38th president of the United States. Ford then delivered the kind of speech that the United States surely needed—candid, sincere, and crafted to ease national tension and clear the air of Watergate.

"You have not elected me as your president by your ballots," said Ford, asking that he be confirmed "with your prayers." "My fellow Americans," he continued, "our long national nightmare is over. Our Constitution works; our great republic is a government of laws and not of men. Here the people rule." Indirectly, he criticized Nixon by stating his belief that "truth is the glue that holds government together." Ford acknowledged that that bond was "strained," both at home and abroad, and described the internal wounds of Watergate as "more painful and more poisonous than those of foreign wars." At the same time, Ford urged that Americans pray for Nixon and his family.

As Ford concluded, there was a lifting of spirits in the East Room and across the nation. Said Senator Mike Mansfield, "It was superb. He hit all the right notes. It was authentic Jerry Ford."

Gerald Ford

Key Dates

1913 — Born on July 14 in Omaha, Nebraska

1941 — Earns law degree at Yale

1948–1973 — Serves as representative to U.S. Congress from Michigan

1965 — Becomes minority leader of the U.S. House of Representatives

1973 — Sworn in as vice president after Spiro Agnew resigns

1974–1976 — Serves as U.S. president after Nixon resigns on August 9

1974 — Grants pardon to Nixon on September 9

2006 — Dies December 26

Focus: Reading for Understanding

1. Under what circumstances did Gerald Ford become president?

2. What did Ford mean when he said: "You have not elected me president by your ballots"? What did he ask of the American people?

3. How did Ford describe the Watergate scandal? What does "The Healing Begins" mean?

4. Word Watch—Look up the following words and note how they are used in the article: *cabinet, strode, administer, oath, excesses, toppling, stately, candid, crafted, republic, acknowledged, bond, internal,* and *authentic.*

Connect

1. Read the profile of Richard Nixon in this collection.

2. What obstacles might Ford face given that he had not been elected president? What advantages might he have? Discuss as a class.

Explore

1. What was the Watergate scandal that forced Nixon's resignation?

2. Why did Ford pardon Nixon? How did the nation react? Find coverage in TIME and other sources.

3. As president, what is the difference between resigning and leaving office after being impeached?

Henry Ford

FIFTEEN CENTS

TIME

The Weekly News-Magazine

HENRY FORD
Riding in many vehicles—
(See Page 5)

VOL. VI. No. 4

JULY 27, 1925

Henry Ford

The father of twentieth-century American industry

July 27, 1925

Henry Ford—who first appeared on TIME's cover in 1925—was selected by the magazine's editors as one of the 100 most important people of the twentieth century. The following reflections on Ford were written in 1998, by Lee Iacocca, president of Ford Motor Company in the 1970s, and later chairman of the Chrysler Corporation.

In September 1946, I was one of 50 college graduates in the training course at the enormous Ford plant near Detroit.

One day, in walked Henry Ford with Charles Lindbergh. They came down my aisle asking men what they were doing. I was working on a mechanical drawing of a clutch spring, and I was worried that they'd ask me a question. I didn't know what the heck I was doing—I'd been there only 30 days. I was just awestruck by the fact that there was Colonel Lindbergh with my new boss, coming to shake my hand.

The boss was a genius. He was an eccentric. He was no prince in his social attitudes and his politics. But Henry Ford's mark in history is almost unbelievable. In 1905, when there were 50 start-up companies a year trying to get into the auto business, his backers at the new Ford Motor Company were insisting that the best way to maximize profits was to build a car for the rich.

But Ford was from modest Michigan farm roots. And he thought that the guys who made the cars ought to be able to afford them so that they too could go for spins on a Sunday afternoon. In typical fashion, instead of listening to his backers, Ford eventually bought them out.

Ford thought that the guys who made the cars ought to be able to afford them.

And that proved to be only the first smart move in a crusade that would make him the father of twentieth-century American industry. When the black Model T rolled out in 1908, it was hailed as America's Everyman car—elegant in its simplicity and a dream machine not just for engineers but for marketing men as well.

When Ford left the family farm at age 16 and walked eight miles to his first job in a Detroit machine shop, only two out of eight Americans lived in the cities. By World War II, that figure would double, and the affordable Model T was one reason for it. People flocked to Detroit for jobs, and if they worked in one of Ford's factories, they could afford one of his cars. By the time production ceased for the Model T in 1927, more than 15 million cars had been sold—or half the world's output.

Henry Ford

Key Dates

1863 — Born near Dearborn, Michigan, on July 30

1879–1902 — Works in machine shops and builds various cars

1903 — Forms Ford Motor Company

1908 — Debuts the Model T, an affordable, instant hit

1913–1914 — Introduces assembly line and $5 daily wage

1918 — Narrowly loses Senate race

1936 — Establishes Ford foundation

1947 — Dies April 7, leaving fortune valued at more than $500 million

Focus: Reading for Understanding

1. Who is Lee Iacocca? Why is he a good choice to write about Henry Ford? How does he describe his former boss?

2. How did Ford disagree with his backers? What did he do instead?

3. Why was the first Model T known as "America's Everyman" car? How did it affect life in America?

4. Word Watch—Look up the following words and note how they are used in the article: *awestruck, eccentric, backers, insisting, maximize, profits, modest, afford, eventually, crusade, hailed, flocked, ceased,* and *output.*

Connect

1. Does anyone come close to being like Ford today? Discuss.

2. How is Ford similar to people like Orville and Wilber Wright, Walt Disney, and Bill Gates?

Explore

1. Research the history of the automobile. Who invented it? What changes in daily life did it bring about (for example, new roads)?

2. Find out more about the Ford Motor Company today. Who are its main competitors?

3. Draw or make a model of your favorite automobile.

Aretha Franklin

Aretha Franklin

Queen of Soul

June 28, 1968

What is soul? Soul comes from the rumble of gospel chords, raw emotion, thumping rhythm, and homey lyrics. For soul personified, there's five feet, five inch Aretha Franklin. Aretha's vocal technique is simple enough: a direct, natural style of delivery that ranges over a full four octaves.

Aretha grew up on the fringe of Detroit's East Side. The Franklin house was a big tree-shaded one, although it did have cockroaches in the kitchen and rats in the basement. Her mother left when Aretha was six and died four years later, two shocks that deeply scarred the shy girl. Her father, Rev. C. L. Franklin, was pastor of Detroit's 4,500-member New Bethel Baptist Church. The preaching there is fiery and emotional. It's not uncommon for parishioners to collapse from the intensity.

> ## "My heart is still there in gospel music. It never left."

Through her father, Aretha became immersed in gospel music. She had her first solo in church at age twelve. Two years later she was touring the country by car as part of her father's gospel show. At eighteen, Aretha decided to try the pop field. The uninspired pop arrangements did not sell well. Deep down, she knew what was wrong with the music: "It wasn't really me." Then, eighteen months ago she switched record labels and began to swing into the soul groove. Her first disk, I Never Loved a Man, sold a million copies. It has been pure success ever since. But only professionally, it seems. Personally, she seems wrapped in sadness. Says veteran gospel singer Mahalia Jackson: "I don't think she's happy." But Aretha says nothing, and others can only speculate.

As a way of finding solace in difficult times, Aretha can always fall back on her heritage. Occasionally, she goes to her father's services to sing a solo. She was there recently. A drenching rain was falling outside, but one thousand parishioners had shown up: Aretha was back.

Moving in front of a lectern, Aretha closed her eyes and sang: "Precious Lord, take my hand . . ." The congregation nodded or swayed gently in their seats. "Sing it!" they cried. Her lines curved out in steadily rising arcs as she let her spirit dictate variations on the lyrics, finally straining upward in pure soul: "Please! Please! Please! Hear my call . . ."

Her voice spiraled down to a breathy whisper, then broke into intense, halting phrases as she almost talked at the end: "Just lead us, lead us, lead us on—We've got to get home."

Afterward, spent and exalted, Lady Soul said something that nobody in the church that night needed to be told: "My heart is still there in gospel music. It never left."

Aretha Franklin

Key Dates

1942 — Born on March 25 in Memphis, Tennessee

1967 — Records first album, which includes the Grammy award winner, "Respect"

1971 — Wins Grammy for best soul gospel performance for "Amazing Grace"

1987 — First woman to be inducted into the Rock and Roll Hall of Fame

1999 — Awarded the Nation Medal of Freedom

2006 — Wins her 19th Grammy award

Focus: Reading for Understanding

1. At what age did Aretha Franklin sing her first solo?

2. Franklin first began singing pop arrangements. How did they fare in the music industry?

3. How many Grammy awards has Franklin won?

4. Word Watch—Look up the following words and note how they are used in the article: *octaves, pop, groove, soul music, solace, heritage, drenching, parishioners, lectern,* and *dictate.*

Connect

Though Franklin has found success professionally, according to some, she has struggled to find happiness in her personal life. Is it possible to be successful and unhappy? Do you know of people who are famous or successful but are unhappy?

Explore

1. What is the Rock and Roll Hall of Fame? Who are some other individuals who have been inducted?

2. Listen to the song, "Respect," "Amazing Grace," or another song by Franklin. Write a review of the song.

Indira Gandhi

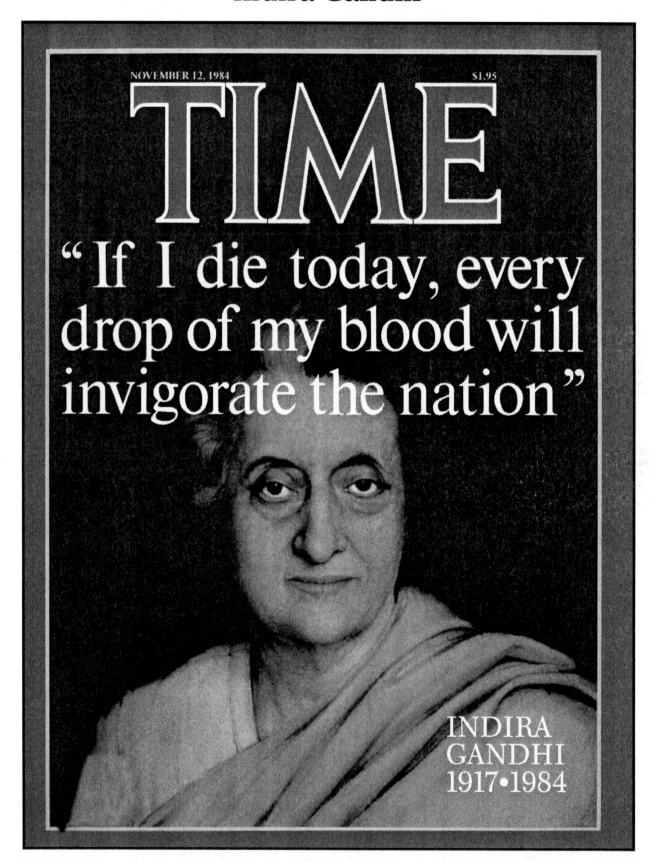

Indira Gandhi

Pays for a bold move with her life

November 12, 1984

Namaste, in Hindi, means "Greetings to you." It is the traditional Indian salutation accompanied by a crossing of hands before the face, as if the speaker were offering a prayer.

At 9:08 last Wednesday morning, Indira Gandhi folded her hands in front of her face, looked at the two guards standing along the path to her office and said, "Namaste." It was to be her last word. Her two body guards took her life. Within hours, India would be plunged into its worst sectarian violence since partition in 1947. As the death toll passed the 1,000 mark, the dominant question was whether the country's new leader, Indira's inexperienced son Rajiv, could, over the long term, sustain the integrity of the ambitious patchwork that against all odds bind 746 million ethnically and religiously diverse people.

It was typical of the proud, stubborn, courageous Indira Gandhi that she hated to wear a bulletproof vest and rarely agreed to do so. Certainly she was a fatalist. The night before her death, she had told a large, enthusiastic crowd in Orissa's capital city, Bhubaneswar, "I am not interested in a long life. I am not afraid of these things. I don't mind if my life goes in the service of this nation. If I die today, every drop of my blood will invigorate the nation."

Like the father of modern India, Mahatma Gandhi, who is not related to her, Indira Gandhi died in a tranquil New Delhi garden, a victim of her country's troubled politics. Mahatma Gandhi was killed in 1948 by a Hindu fanatic enraged by concessions made to the Muslims and by the partition of India and Pakistan. Mrs. Gandhi's murderers were Sikhs, whose religious community of 15 million represents only about 2% of India's population but holds an important place in the country's life.

> # Like the father of modern India before her, she died a victim of her country's troubled politics.

Last June, after failing to quell the Sikh's desire for greater autonomy and put an end to an extremist movement for an independent Sikh nation, Mrs. Gandhi had sent the army into Punjab and into the most sacred of all Sikh shrines. Sikh fanatics had turned the Golden Temple into a sort of holy fortress. At least 600 people, including the radical leader of Sikhs, were killed in the battle that occurred. Mrs. Gandhi's move was a bold step and she probably paid for it with her life.

Indira Gandhi

Key Dates

1917 — Born on November 19, in Northern India

1942 — Marries Feroze Gandhi

1947 — India wins independence from Great Britain

1959 — Becomes president of India's Congress

1964 — Lal Bhadur Shartri becomes prime minister

1966 — Shartri dies, Congress votes Gandhi as prime minister of India

1977 — Loses her seat in Parliament

1980 — Reelected prime minister

1984 — Killed by two of her bodyguards on October 31

Focus: Reading for Understanding

1. What does *Namaste* mean in Hindi?

2. How did Indira Gandhi die? Why is her death compared to the death of Mahatma Gandhi, father of India?

3. What did Gandhi feel were the responsibilities that came with her position? How did she use her role for the good of the country?

4. Word Watch—Look up the following words and note how they are used in the article: *salutation, sectarian, ambitious, fatalist, quell, autonomy, ethnically, fanatic, invigorate,* and *dominant.*

Connect

1. Gandhi had strong convictions about her country and her beliefs. About which topics do you feel strongly? With whom do you share these convictions? Share your ideas with the class.

2. Gandhi said she was willing to die for her convictions and beliefs. What do you think of this? Can you think of other people who have died for the good of their country or cause?

Explore

1. Look up India on a map. Research the country. What are the conditions of India today? What is the condition of the government?

2. Compare and contrast Gandhi with Corazon Aquino. Did they have the same leadership style? How are they different and how are they alike?

Mohandas Gandhi

Mohandas Gandhi

His weapon was nonviolence.

January 5, 1931

Mohandas Gandhi was TIME's "Man of the Year" in 1930. In 1999, the magazine's editors selected him as one of the three most influential people of the twentieth century, along with Albert Einstein and Franklin Roosevelt. An excerpt from the 1999 article appears below.

In a century marked by brutality, Mohandas Gandhi perfected a method of bringing about change, one that turned out to have more lasting impact. The words do not translate readily into English: Satyagraha (holding onto the deepest truth and soul-force) and ahimsa (the love remaining when thoughts of violence are dispelled). They formed the basis for civil disobedience and nonviolent resistance. "Nonviolence is the greatest force at the disposal of mankind. It is mightier than the mightiest weapon of destruction devised by the ingenuity of man."

"Nonviolence is the greatest force at the disposal of mankind."

Gandhi became not just a political force but a spiritual guide for those repelled by the hate and greed that polluted this century. "Generations to come," said Albert Einstein, "will scarce believe that such a one as this ever in flesh and blood walked upon this earth."

Gandhi's life of civil disobedience began while he was a young lawyer in South Africa. Because he was a dark-skinned Indian, he was told to move to a third-class seat on a train even though he held a first-class ticket. He refused. When he was 61, he and his followers marched 240 miles in 24 days to make their own salt from the sea in defiance of British colonial laws and taxes. Several thousand had joined his march. More than 60,000 were eventually arrested, including Gandhi.

Gandhi did not see the full realization of his dreams. India finally gained independence from Britain in 1947, but a civil war between Hindus and Muslims resulted, despite his efforts, in the bloody birth of Pakistan. A Hindu fanatic killed Gandhi, on his way to prayers.

Gandhi's spirit and philosophy, however, transformed the century. His most notable heir was Martin Luther King Jr., who began studying Gandhi in college. King was initially skeptical about the use of nonviolence. But by the time of the Montgomery bus boycott, he later wrote, "I had come to see early that the Christian doctrine of love operating through the Gandhian method of nonviolence was one of the most potent weapons available to the Negro in his struggle for freedom." The bus boycott, sit-ins, freedom rides and, above all, the 1965 Selma march with its bloody Sunday on the Edmund Pettus Bridge showed how right he, and Gandhi, were.

Mohandas Gandhi

Key Dates

1869 — Born in Porbandar, India, on October 2

1893 — Goes to South Africa and battles for the rights of Indians

1915–1920 — Begins his struggle for India's independence

1930 — Leads hundreds on a long Salt March to Dandi to protest a tax on salt

1947 — Negotiates an end to 190 years of British colonial rule in India

1948 — Killed by a fanatic opposed to Gandhi's tolerance of other religions

Focus: Reading for Understanding

1. What is civil disobedience? When and why did Mohandas Gandhi use this tactic? What were the results?

2. What does Gandhi mean when he states that nonviolence "is mightier than the mightiest weapon of destruction"? What is your reaction to this statement? How does the cover pose reflect his philosophy?

3. How did Gandhi influence Martin Luther King Jr.?

4. Word Watch—Look up the following words and note how they are used in the article: *brutality, dispelled, destruction, ingenuity, repelled, desolate, culminated, defiance, skeptical, potent,* and *boycott.*

Connect

1. Do you share Gandhi's idea that "nonviolence is the greatest force"? Or do you think wars and violence are necessary to bring about social change?

2. Read about Martin Luther King Jr., Albert Einstein, and Franklin Roosevelt. Did they agree with Gandhi's ideas of nonviolence?

Explore

Martin Luther King Jr. and others staged many nonviolent protests, as the article reports. Learn more about the Montgomery bus boycott, sit-ins, freedom rides, or the march from Selma.

Bill Gates

FASHION MAGS: DIRTY LAUNDRY

TIME

Master Of the Universe

Having conquered the world's computers, BILL GATES takes aim at banks, phone companies, even Hollywood. He's in for the fight of his life.

Bill Gates
America's software tycoon

June 5, 1995

At age 39, Bill Gates, the founder of *Microsoft®*, seems to have achieved the Information Age's equivalent of the American Dream. Through intelligence, ruthlessness, and hard work, he dominates a technology so important to modern life that it touches nearly every office, school, and desktop.

He dominates a technology so important to modern life that it touches nearly every office, school, and desktop.

How big is *Microsoft*? Eight out of 10 of the world's personal computers could not boot up (that is to say, start) if it were not for *Microsoft's* software programs. What is even more impressive—not to mention profitable—is that the company also dominates the market for almost every big-ticket application program, like word processing. Financially, the company couldn't be stronger. *Microsoft's* revenues last year were nearly $5 billion, more than all its competitors' combined. It employs 16,400 people—one-third of them women—in 49 countries. Thousands of current and former *Microsoft* employees have become millionaires, at least on paper, and three are billionaires.

Gates has a net worth of more than $10 billion, making him the richest man in America. He was married last year on the Hawaiian island of Lanai. He is building a $40 million-plus home on suburban Seattle's Lake Washington, with video "walls" to display an ever-changing collection of electronic art, a trampoline room with a 25-ft. vaulted ceiling where he can burn off steam, a 20-car underground garage, and a trout stream.

How does he do it? The computer-software business is always changing, and nobody navigates this chaos better than Gates, who not only understands the technology (he wrote the company's first product, *Microsoft BASIC* but also meets regularly with the heads of all the major computer firms. This enables him to spot trends and see what is ahead as clearly as anyone in the industry. It is as if he were playing 3-D tic-tac-toe in a world where everyone else is playing in 2-D.

"You get Bill Gates in a room with his peers and he will know more than anybody else in the room," says Nathan Myhrvold, a *Microsoft* vice president. This gives the company a big edge. "If you want to surf the wave of technology, you put someone on the board who knows how to surf," he says.

Under Gates' direction, *Microsoft* is the undisputed leader in a business now crucial to everybody's life. What *Microsoft* has yet to discover—and what the world is waiting to learn—is whether the qualities that brought about its triumphs will be able to keep it on top.

Bill Gates

Key Dates

1955 — Born in Seattle on October 28

1975 — Drops out of Harvard College to cofound *Microsoft*

1980 — Licenses MS-DOS to IBM for its first personal computer

1986 — Becomes billionaire at age 31 with public sale of company stock

1990 — Releases *Windows* 3.0

1995–1996 — Introduces *Windows 95* and *Internet Explorer* browser for the Net age

1998 — Justice Department files antitrust suit against *Microsoft*

Focus: Reading for Understanding

1. How is Bill Gates described? Cite specific words and phrases.

2. What statistical evidence does the writer provide to illustrate that *Microsoft* dominates the technology market?

3. What does the writer feel is the secret of Gates' success?

4. Word Watch—Look up the following words and note how they are used in the article: *founder, ruthlessness, dominates, profitable, big-ticket, application, financially, revenues, competitor, employees, net worth, suburban, chaos, trends, peers, undisputed,* and *antitrust*.

Connect

1. Do you use a computer? For what? Imagine a time before personal computers became so common.

2. What are the pros and cons of personal computer use?

3. If you became a millionaire, what would you do? Does great wealth carry a responsibility to society?

Explore

1. Since 1995, Gates has given away millions of dollars. Find out how he has chosen to share his wealth.

2. Learn more about the antitrust suit against *Microsoft*. Why did the U.S. government sue *Microsoft*?

Althea Gibson

Althea Gibson

A trailblazer on and off the tennis court

August 26, 1957

Althea Gibson, who began her career playing paddle tennis on the streets, was the first African American player ever to be invited to the U.S. Lawn Tennis Association national championships, held in Forest Hills, New York. She is still only a tolerated stranger in Forest Hills locker rooms. But now, none of that matters. For Gibson has finally whipped the one opponent that could keep her down: her own self-doubt. At 30, an age when most athletes have eased over to the far slope of their careers, Gibson has begun the last, steep climb.

> **"If I have any ambition, it's to be the best woman tennis player who ever lived."**

Sent abroad by the State Department in 1955 as an athletic ambassador, Gibson made friends and won tournaments from Naples to New Delhi. In Paris last year, she won the French championship, her first big-time title. At Wimbledon, her new-found confidence carried her all the way to the quarter-finals before she faltered. This year, she won at Wimbledon and came home a queen, owner of tennis' brightest crown.

Lean, tall, and well-muscled (5 feet 10½ inches, 144 lbs.), Althea Gibson is not the most graceful figure on the court, and her game is not the most stylish. But, her tennis has a champion's unmistakable power and drive. Says tennis champ Tony Trabert: "She hits the ball hard and plays like a man. She runs and covers the court better than any of the other women."

When Gibson left for Wimbledon in May, only three close friends were at the airport to wish her luck. When she returned a winner, Idlewild Airport was awash with people. New York City honored her with a ticker-tape parade. And people breathlessly wanted to know how it had felt to shake hands with Queen Elizabeth at Wimbledon and what they had said to each other. (The Queen: "It was a very enjoyable match, but you must have been very hot on the court." Gibson: "I hope it wasn't as hot in the royal box.")

During a lunch given her by New York's mayor, Gibson made a moving speech. "God grant that I wear this crown I have won with dignity," she said. "I just can't describe the joy in my heart." Later, she looked ahead to her future and said, "I don't see why I can't play till I'm 35. If I have any ambition, it's to be the best woman tennis player who ever lived."

Althea Gibson

Key Dates

1927 — Born in Silver, South Carolina, on August 25

1948 — Wins the first of 10 straight national championships run by the American Tennis Association

1950 — Becomes the first African American player to compete in the grass-court championships at Forest Hills, New York

1957, 1958 — Wins both Wimbledon and U.S. Nationals singles championships

1958 — Publishes autobiography, *I Always Wanted To Be Somebody*

1971 — Named to the National Lawn Tennis Hall of Fame

2003 — Dies in New Jersey on September 28

Focus: Reading for Understanding

1. Explain what the writer means in stating that Althea Gibson is "still only a tolerated stranger in Forest Hills locker rooms." What was going on in the country in terms of racial segregation?

2. How does the writer describe Gibson and her style of tennis? Note the use of quotations from an outside source.

3. What is Gibson's goal? What is your ambition?

4. Word Watch—Look up the following words and note how they are used in the article: *trailblazer, tolerated, opponent, ambassador, tournament, faltered,* and *dignity*.

Connect

1. Do you or does anyone you know play tennis? Do you know any of the rules and vocabulary of the game?

2. According to the article, Gibson defeated a difficult opponent: her own self-doubt. Do you have any self-doubts? About what? Have you conquered other doubts in the past? How?

Explore

Other pioneers who have broken barriers have appeared on TIME's cover. They include Jackie Robinson, Sandra Day O'Connor, and Margaret Thatcher. As a group, brainstorm the pros and cons of being a first. Identify another pioneer and learn more about his or her life and work.

Mikhail Gorbachev

Mikhail Gorbachev

He unleashed democracy in Eastern Europe.

January 1, 1990

The people of the Soviet Union longed for a leader with energy and vision, someone who would represent their pride rather than their shame. So, there was a national murmur of interest in 1979, when the country got its first look at Mikhail Sergeyevich Gorbachev at a televised awards ceremony. Not only did this new Central Committee Secretary, then 48 years of age, seem at ease among the much older group of party elders; he was the only one able to say thank you for his medal without reading from an index card.

Since his selection as head of the Communist Party in 1985, Gorbachev has exceeded both the hopes of those who longed for change in the Soviet Union and the fears of those, no doubt including comrades who voted for him, who worried that he would threaten the power and privileges of the elite in the country. He has been a political powerhouse, showering sparks inside and outside the country. He is committed to perestroika, an effort to make the economy produce what the people want to consume, and glasnost, an end to official lying by the government and the beginning of a more open society. These two ideas have changed the Soviet Union and made possible enormous changes for other countries as well.

What were long called, and accurately so, the "satellite," or captive, nations of Eastern Europe (Poland, Hungary, East Germany, Czechoslovakia) are carrying out revolutions of their own and moving toward western-style democracy. They are doing so because Gorbachev is letting them. In the USSR the old order is not just passing; it is already on what the Russian Revolutionary Leon Trotsky called the trash heap of history. No one, certainly including Gorbachev, knows what is coming next. But whatever it is, it will be something new.

"Any nation has the right to decide its fate by itself."

Historians debate whether great forces or great men move the world. By unleashing the forces of democracy, Gorbachev gave new support to the theory that it is great men. He may not be able to control the forces of change himself. They could even sweep him away. But no matter what happens next in the great Eurasian landmass where 1.8 billion people live under Communism—and no matter what happens to Gorbachev—he has established his place in history as the catalyst of a new European reality. "Any nation has the right to decide its fate by itself," he said last month. It is one thing for the most powerful Communist on earth to speak those words. It is momentous when he not only means them but also puts them into practice.

Mikhail Gorbachev

Key Dates

1931 — Born in Privolnoye, in southern Russia, on March 2

1985 — Elected General Secretary of the Communist Party of the Soviet Union

1986 — Initiates a period of political openness (*glasnost*) and transformation (*perestroika*) to modernize the USSR

1990 — Awarded the Nobel Peace Prize

1990–1991 — President of Soviet Union until its dismantlement

1991 — Resigns from office and retires from public life

Focus: Reading for Understanding

1. What first impression did Mikhail Gorbachev make in 1979 as Central Committee Secretary? In 1985 as head of the Communist Party?

2. What do *perestroika* and *glasnost* mean? How have these ideas affected both Russia and other Eastern European nations?

3. Why do you think Gorbachev was chosen not "Man of the Year" but "Man of the Decade" by TIME?

4. Word Watch—Look up the following words and note how they are used in the article: *murmur, party elders, exceeded, comrades, elite, powerhouse, consume, satellite, revolutions, unleashing, catalyst,* and *momentous.*

Connect

1. "Historians debate whether great forces or great men move the world." Hold your own class debate on this question.

2. Choose one of the profiles in this collection. Write an essay about the statement above using the person you chose as an example.

Explore

1. What happened when the USSR was dismantled? What is happening in Russian government today? How far have the reforms begun by Gorbachev progressed?

2. Find out more about the Communist Party and revolutionary leader Leon Trotsky.

Alex Haley

Alex Haley

Haley's Prescription: Talk, Write, Reunite

February 14, 1977

At his home outside Los Angeles, every mail delivery brings bulging sacks of letters to Alex Haley—all of it evidence of the astonishing impact produced by his saga of a family's tortuous trail to freedom. Haley thinks he knows why *Roots* touched all Americans.

"In this country," says Alex Haley, "we are young, brash, and technologically oriented. We are all trying to build machines so that we can push a button and get things done a millisecond faster. But as a consequence, we are drawing away from one of the most priceless things we have—where we came from and how we got to be where we are. The young are drawing away from the older people."

Haley quickly grants that television can be a "positive social influence," but then he goes on to blame the tube for widening the generation gap. "TV has contributed to the elimination of the old form of entertainment where the family sat around listening to older people. TV has alienated youth from its elders, and this has cost us culturally and socially."

The universal appeal of *Roots*, he feels, is based on the average American's longing for a sense of heritage. Haley even goes so far as to advocate an antidote to this trend toward rootlessness. Young people can "revolutionize" their own roles within their families, he says, and he offers them a three-point prescription. "I tell young people to go to the oldest members of their family and get as much oral history as possible. Many grandparents carry three or four generations of history in their heads but don't talk about it because they've been ignored. And when the young person starts doing this, the old are warmed to the cockles of their souls and will tell everything they can muster."

"There is something magic about the common sense of a family bond."

Then, Haley says, the history of the family should be written and a copy sent to every member. Haley encourages youths to rummage through attics, basements, and closets for illuminating family letters and other memorabilia. "It's a simple thing," says Haley. "But the existence of a written history gives the family something it never had before. There is an almost miraculous effect once it exists." Finally, Haley urges, "Have family reunions. There is something magic about the common sense of a family bond. The reunion gives a sense that the family cares about itself and is proud of itself. And there is the assumption that you, the family member, are obligated to reflex this pride, and if possible, add to it."

Alex Haley

Key Dates

1921 — Born on August 11

1965 — *The Autobiography of Malcolm X* is published

1976 — After 11 years of research, *Roots* is published

1977 — Wins National Book Award and Pulitzer Prize for *Roots*; receives NAACP's Spingarn Medal

1992 — Dies on February 10

Focus: Reading for Understanding

1. What does Alex Haley think has contributed to the widening of the generation gap?

2. What awards did Haley receive for his book *Roots*?

3. What does Haley advise about families? Family reunions? Family history?

4. Word Watch—Look up the following words and note how they are used in the article: *alienated, advocate, antidote, cockles, rummage, illuminating,* and *memorabilia.*

Connect

1. Have a class debate about the status of families today. Discuss whether TV and other distractions alienate the youth from their elders.

2. Interview a grandparent to find out about your family history. What did you learn about your family? Share your findings with the class.

Explore

1. Haley wrote *The Autobiography of Malcom X.* Who is Malcom X? What is an autobiography?

2. If possible, watch the movie version of *Roots* and write a review. If time permits, read the book *Roots* and compare it to the movie.

Adolf Hitler

Adolf Hitler

A dictator who preached hatred

May 7, 1945

Fate knocked at the door last week for Europe's two fascist dictators. Benito Mussolini, shot in the back and through the head, lay dead in Milan. And Adolf Hitler had been buried in the rubble of his collapsing Third Reich. Hitler's total war against non-German mankind was ending in total defeat. Around him, the Third Reich, which was to have lasted 1,000 years, sank.

All that was certain to remain after 1,000 years was the all-but-incredible story of the demonic little man who rose from a gutter to make himself absolute master of most of Europe. The suffering that he brought about was beyond human power to compute. The bodies of his victims were heaped across Europe from Stalingrad to London. In his concentration camps, incinerators raged night and day to burn the bodies of those he had condemned to death. The ruin in terms of human lives was forever incalculable. It had required a coalition of the whole world to destroy him.

How had it happened? Who was this monster? Failing even the most elementary studies, Hitler grew up a half-educated man, untrained for any profession. Following the deaths of his parents, Hitler packed his few clothes and set out for Vienna, where he was twice rejected from painting school. Encountering Jews for the first time, he was swayed by the publications of Vienna's violently anti-Semitic Mayor Doktor Karl Lueger. Soon young Hitler had concluded that the Jew was the enemy of all mankind—and the particular enemy of the Germans.

Hitler's political career began in 1919 when he became member No. 7 of a tiny political party. He found an economic program in the scrambled theories of another member. And he found something much more important—his voice. One night a visitor said some friendly words about Jews. Without thinking twice, Hitler burst forth in a speech dripping with hatred. He had become an orator. Soon he became the party's leader, changed its name to the National Socialist German Labor Party—Nazi for short—and wrote its anti-Semitic, antidemocratic program.

The suffering that he brought about was beyond human power to compute.

Then, Hitler made one of the most valuable mistakes of his life: he and his handful of party comrades decided to seize the Bavarian government. The plot failed, and Hitler went to jail in the Landsberg prison.

While in prison, with the help of Rudolf Hess, he wrote *Mein Kampf* (My Struggle). The book included the plans for Hitler's aggression against Germany and the rest of the world, as well as his intense hatred of Jews. Seldom in the course of human history has a plotter set forth his purposes in plainer language or more explicit detail.

Adolf Hitler

Key Dates

1889 — Born in Braunau, Austria, on April 20

1919 — Helps form the Nazi Party

1924 — Writes *Mein Kampf* in prison

1933 — Becomes dictator of Germany and prepares the nation for a "Final Solution of the Jewish Problem"

1939 — Invades Poland and starts World War II

1945 — Commits suicide. Historians report that some 11 million people, including six million Jews, were murdered under Hitler's regime.

Focus: Reading for Understanding

1. What happened to dictators Mussolini and Adolf Hitler in 1945? How does the cover reflect this?

2. Describe Hitler's background. When he moved to Vienna, how did he become prejudiced against Jewish people? How did this hatred intensify and express itself later on?

3. How did Hitler begin his political career? What was his first oration?

4. What did Hitler write in prison? What was it about?

5. Word Watch—Look up the following words and note how they are used in the article: *fascist, dictator, Third Reich, demonic, concentration camps, incinerators, condemned, coalition, swayed, anti-Semitic, theories, orator, antidemocratic, comrades, seldom,* and *explicit.*

Connect

1. What do you know about the Holocaust? Brainstorm as a class.

2. Does anti-Semitism still exist? What other kinds of prejudice exist? How can we combat them?

Explore

What were conditions like for Jewish people in Nazi Germany? Read *The Diary of Anne Frank,* a first-person account of a young Jewish girl's life in hiding.

David Ho

TIME
MAN OF THE YEAR

DR. DAVID HO

AIDS
RESEARCHER

David Ho

Language and cultural differences were not obstacles.

December 30, 1996

TIME's 1996 "Man of the Year" was born in Taiwan on November 3, 1952. At birth, he was given the name Da-I, which means "Great One." It is a name reflecting great expectations. To forge a better life for his family, Ho's father moved to America. For nine years, Da-I would know his father only through letters.

"You always retain a bit of an underdog mentality."

For Da-I and his younger brother, the years of waiting were filled with long school days that included "cram school" for extra tutoring. Street stickball was a welcome interruption. And whenever he could, Da-I would leaf through comic books.

When his father sent for the family, a seriousness came over Da-I. The 12-year-old packed his own bags and stayed awake throughout the flight to watch over his mother and younger brother. They were traveling to a land they did not know and whose language they did not speak. It would be a place where they would receive new names and new identities. Their father had picked the boys' American names from the Bible. Thus, it came to pass that Ho Dai-I became David Ho. His younger brother became Phillip.

His father instructed his wife that their sons were to stick to Taiwanese and Mandarin Chinese and not learn English until they got to America for a better chance of speaking it without an accent. As Ho's mother recalls in careful but imperfect English, "When we first come to U.S., we don't know any words. David would come home from school and say, 'I don't know what they talking about.'" Says David: "We hadn't even learned the ABCs. I remember being laughed at by classmates who thought I was dumb."

David did two things: he became an introvert and stuck close to the family. He focused on school and achievement, earning all A's. Six months after starting school, David settled into the language, thanks to an English-as-a-second-language program and the miracle of TV. "We watched *The Three Stooges,*" Phillip says."

Medicine was David's second choice as a career. After high school, he attended MIT and CalTech as a physics major. Then, he made his way to Harvard Medical School. Soon enough, medicine provided the turning point of his career. His mother recalls, "He told me he saw a lot of young people die. He say that must be some disease, so he want to keep researching to find out why." Ho had met up with HIV.

Ho credits his success to immigrant drive: "People get to this new world and they want to carve out their place in it. The result is dedication and a higher level of work ethic." He adds, "You always retain a bit of an underdog mentality." And if they work hard and lie low long enough, even underdogs have their day.

David Ho

Key Dates

1952 — Born in Taichung, Taiwan, on November 3

1956 — Ho's father moves to America

1965 — Ho and his mother and brother join his father in America

1974–1980 — Attends Harvard Medical School

1987–1990 — Begins research at UCLA that leads to a better understanding of how HIV attacks the body; leads to more effective treatments

1990 — Aaron Diamond Center to study HIV/AIDS is founded; Ho is named as director

Focus: Reading for Understanding

1. Where was David Ho born? At what age did he come with his family to the United States?

2. What was Ho's first career choice? Second career choice?

3. What was the transition from Taiwan to the United States like for Ho?

4. Word Watch—Look up the following words and note how they are used in the article: *frenzied, introvert, immigrant drive, work ethic, parcel post, eerie, tutoring, identities,* and *underdog.*

Connect

David Ho had a difficult time in a new country with a new language. Have you ever tried to learn a new language? Learn 10 words in a different language and try to use them to communicate.

Explore

1. Ho was named TIME's "Man of the Year" because of his work with the virus that causes AIDS. Make a list of other men who have been named TIME's "Man of the Year." Why have they been named? Have there been any women named?

2. Ho attended MIT. What type of school is this? What significant individuals or inventions have been associated with MIT?

Jesse Jackson

Jesse Jackson

A preacher who ran for president

April 11, 1988

Any American child can grow up to be president. That is one of the basic principles of democracy, but through the generations, it has become a kindergarten fable. Adults, of course, know the truth. The presidency is reserved for white men who have held high office and who have almost always avoided embracing a cause or expressing a sentiment that is far outside the mainstream.

For the first time in the nation's history, a major political party was grappling with one of the biggest what-ifs of all: What if Democratic voters actually nominate an African American man for president?

But there are rare moments when the truths that seemed self-evident begin to be reexamined. It is a slow process, and it does not always immediately lead to dramatic consequences. Still, just the act of toying with a previously unimaginable possibility leaves a mark. Even if the surface of life goes on pretty much as before, a seed has been planted that may someday bloom.

And so it is in the spring of 1988 with the campaign of Jesse Jackson, twenty years after the assassination of the Reverend Martin Luther King Jr. Jackson was not only one of King's aides; he was the rebel in King's official family. He was the one who appeared on television the day after the shooting wearing a bloody shirt and boldly—and inaccurately—claiming that it was he, Jesse, who cradled the dying Martin in his arms.

Now exactly two decades after the death of the man who fought for the right to vote, Jackson is demanding the political rights that come with those votes. And so, for the first time in the nation's history, a major political party was grappling with one of the biggest what-ifs of all: What if Democratic voters actually nominate an African American man for president?

That question would be explosive if the contender were a safe token, a man who differed only by the accident of his race. But this contender challenges all the established expectations at once. For Jackson, the son of a teenage mother, is a fiery preacher who rose to national prominence through controversy.

Such a nomination would have been unthinkable four years ago. Indeed, it was unthinkable just two weeks ago. But polls showed Jackson running neck and neck with Democratic party favorite Michael Dukakis.

Even if Jackson does not ultimately leave the Democratic Convention in triumph, he will still be a victor. For he has already taught white America that an African American person is not only somebody, he can be anybody. Even president.

Jesse Jackson

Key Dates

1941 — Born in Greenville, South Carolina, on October 8

1963 — Arrested in civil rights protest in Greensboro, North Carolina

1968 — Ordained a Baptist minister

1984 — Founds and becomes president of the Rainbow Coalition, a position he still holds

1984, 1988 — Runs for U.S. presidency

1999 — Helps secure the release of three American military prisoners from Yugoslavia

Focus: Reading for Understanding

1. Why does the writer say that it is a "kindergarten fable" to believe that any child in America can grow up to be president?

2. How did Jesse Jackson challenge political ideas in America? What kind of candidate usually runs for president?

3. What was Jackson fighting for in 1988? Define his relationship to King.

4. Explain the punctuation used on the cover.

5. Word Watch—Look up the following words and note how they are used in the article: *principles, embracing, mainstream, toying, previously, unimaginable, inaccurately, grappling, nominate, contender, prominence, controversy, unthinkable,* and *victor.*

Connect

1. Do you believe anyone can grow up to be president of the United States? Have a class debate.

2. Find out about Martin Luther King Jr. and Marian Anderson. What are the similarities and differences of these profiles with Jackson's?

Explore

1. What happened at the National Democratic Convention in 1988?

2. What is the Rainbow Coalition? What is its role today?

Lyndon B. Johnson

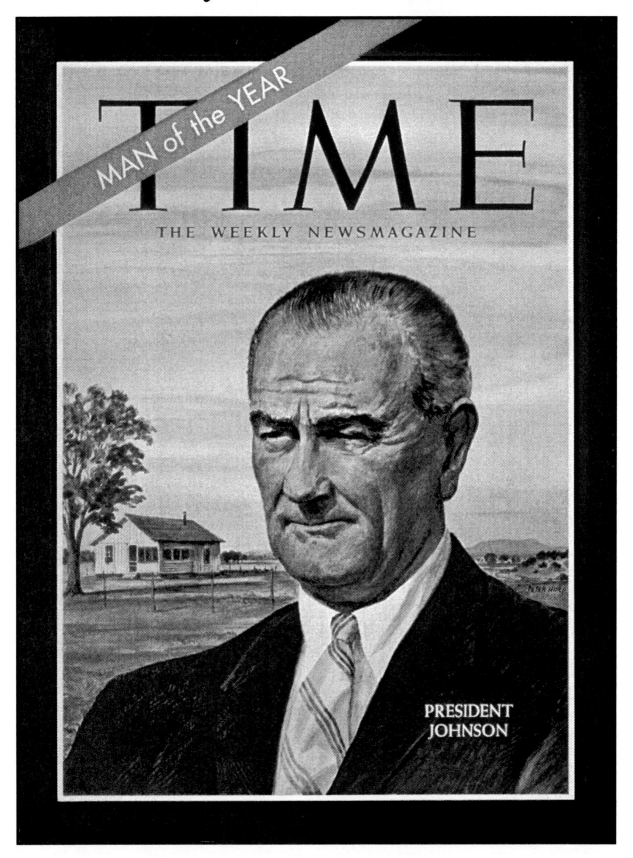

MAN of the YEAR

TIME

THE WEEKLY NEWSMAGAZINE

PRESIDENT
JOHNSON

Lyndon B. Johnson

He won the biggest election triumph in history.

January 1, 1965

In November 1963, Lyndon Baines Johnson became president following the assassination of John F. Kennedy. Nearly a year later, Johnson defeated Republican Barry Goldwater in the 1964 presidential race, winning the biggest election triumph in U.S. history. The year 1964 was truly Johnson's year—his to act in, his to mold, his to dominate.

"I want to be president of all the people."

And dominate it he did. By words and gestures, by pleas and orders, by speeches noble and blunt, but most of all by work. He worked in the White House, at the ranch, on the Hill, on the stump, in his limousine (with four separate communication setups) and aboard the jet (with $2 million in electronic gear). He worked by letter, wire, scrambler, and hot line. He worked in the bath and in the bedroom, at every meal and over every drink.

He astonished his supporters with his energy ("The Whirlwind President") and surprised the skeptics by surpassing almost all of his predecessors in first-year accomplishments.

In that brief span, he:

- Put into effect a new relationship with the other "coequal" branches of government, thus achieving the truest partnership with Congress—in the checks-and-balances sense described by the Constitution—in well over a century. His remarkable legislative record was crowned by the historic Civil Rights Act of 1964. It was the strongest civil rights legislation ever passed by Congress.

- Worked constantly to win business confidence without losing labor's confidence. The result: increased national prosperity. Johnson also succeeded in getting an $11.5 billion tax cut through Congress.

- Pursued the goal of world peace while keeping U.S. prestige high and U.S. power strong. He provided no instant answers, but he met his major crisis—that of the Gulf of Tonkin—with just about the proper mixture of force and caution.

- Worked tirelessly to achieve a national consensus, with two phrases—"Let us reason together" and "I want to be president of all the people." The consensus, of course, became his on November 3 with the greatest electoral victory since 1936 and the largest percent (61%) of the popular vote ever.

Lyndon B. Johnson

Key Dates

1908 — Born in Stonewall, Texas, on August 27

1948 — Elected to the U.S. Senate

1960 — Becomes vice president when John F. Kennedy is elected president

1963 — Becomes the 36th president following Kennedy's assassination

1964 — Defeats Barry Goldwater in the presidential race. LBJ is highly successful in getting his civil rights and "Great Society" legislation passed, but his work on domestic issues is later overshadowed by the Vietnam War.

1973 — Dies in Texas on January 22

Focus: Reading for Understanding

1. Under what circumstances did Lyndon Johnson become president? How did he prove that he was popular and talented in his own right?

2. Why was Johnson called the "Whirlwind President"? What did he accomplish in his first year in office?

3. What did Johnson mean when he said, "I want to be president of all the people"?

4. Word Watch—Look up the following words and note how they are used in the article: *assassination, defeated, dominate, blunt, the Hill, stump, scrambler, whirlwind, skeptics, surpassing, predecessors, coequal, legislative, crowned, prosperity, prestige, tirelessly, consensus,* and *electoral.*

Connect

If you were running for president, what would your campaign slogan be? Draw a campaign poster and put the posters up in your classroom. Then, take a vote!

Explore

1. Research the system of political "checks and balances" in the United States government. Draw a chart to illustrate the different branches.

2. Find out more about key events in Johnson's term: the Gulf of Tonkin incident, the Civil Rights Act of 1964, the Great Society and the Vietnam War. How did these events shape public opinion of him?

John F. Kennedy

John F. Kennedy

He brought youthful energy to Washington.

January 5, 1962

The taste of victory was fresh and sweet to John Fitzgerald (Jack) Kennedy. Just about a year ago, he sat in the drawing room of his Georgetown home and spoke breezily about the office he would assume. "Sure it's a big job," he said. "But I don't know anybody who can do it any better than I can. I'm going to be in it for four years. It isn't going to be so bad. You've got time to think—and besides, the pay is pretty good."

One year later, on a cool, grey day, the 35th president of the United States sat at his desk in the Oval Office of the White House and discussed the same subject. "This job is interesting," he said in that combination of Irish slur and Bostonese that has become immediately identifiable on all the world's radios, "but the possibilities for trouble are unlimited. It represents a chance to exercise your judgment on matters of importance. It takes a lot of thought and effort. It's been a tough first year, but then they're all going to be tough."

The words, not particularly memorable, might have come from any of a thousand thoughtful executives after a year on the job. But here they were spoken by the still-young executive in the world's biggest job. And they showed the difference in attitude and tone that twelve months in the White House have worked on John F. Kennedy.

Jack Kennedy—"Man of the Year" for 1961—had passionately sought the presidency. The closeness of his victory did not disturb him; he took over the office with a youth-can-do-anything sort of self-confidence. He learned better; but learn he did. And in so doing he not only made 1961 the most endlessly interesting and exciting presidential year within recent memory; he also made the process of his growing up to be president a saving factor for the United States in the cold war.

"The torch has been passed to a new generation of Americans."

Kennedy has always had a way with the people—a style that swings with grace from high formality to almost prankish casualness, a quick charm, the patience to listen, a sure social touch, and an interest in knowledge.

Kennedy's eloquence—and a spirit of hope that is based on confidence—was unmistakable in his inaugural address, delivered under a brilliant sun after a night of snow. "Let the word go forth from this time and place, to friend and foe alike, that the torch has been passed to a new generation of Americans," he said. "In the long history of the world, only a few generations have been granted the role of defending freedom in its hour of maximum danger. I do not shrink from this responsibility—I welcome it."

Such was Kennedy's performance during the inauguration ceremonies that the late Speaker of the House Sam Rayburn was moved to remark: "He is a man of destiny."

John F. Kennedy

Key Dates

1917 — Born in Boston, Massachusetts, on May 29

1943 — Survives crash of torpedo boat in Pacific

1952 — Elected senator

1960 — Defeats Richard Nixon to become 35th president

1961 — Commits major resources to space exploration, vowing that a man would walk on the moon by 1970

1963 — Dies in Dallas, Texas, on November 22, the fourth U.S. president to be assassinated

Focus: Reading for Understanding

1. How did John Kennedy feel about becoming 35th president of the United States? How did he feel a year later?

2. How does the writer describe Kennedy's personality?

3. Read the quotations from Kennedy's inaugural address out loud. Explain the meaning in your own words. What was the "maximum danger"?

4. Rayburn could not have known that Kennedy would be assassinated when he called him a "man of destiny." Think about this description and Kennedy's enthusiasm in this light.

5. Word Watch—Look up the following words and note how they are used in the article: *breezily, slur, executives, passionately, sought, factor, cold war, prankish, eloquence, inaugural, address, foe, generation, granted, defending, maximum,* and *destiny.*

Connect

Ask your parents or grandparents for their memories of JFK, his presidency, assassination, and family.

Explore

What was the "Camelot" period of Kennedy's presidency? Where did this name come from?

Martin Luther King Jr.

Martin Luther King Jr.

He led a revolution for equality.

January 3, 1964

In 1963, TIME selected Martin Luther King Jr. as its "Man of the Year," declaring him "the symbol of a revolution." King had led protests in Birmingham, Alabama, where city officials tried to uphold segregation by unleashing police dogs and fire hoses on peaceful protesters. In August 1963, King inspired Americans with his "I Have a Dream" speech, delivered at the March on Washington.

The March on Washington was a remarkable spectacle. More than 200,000 people—whites and blacks of all ages—walked from the Washington Monument to the Lincoln Memorial. There, a variety of civil-rights leaders spoke.

> **"When we let freedom ring, all of God's children will be able to join hands and sing, 'Free at last.'"**

But it was Martin Luther King Jr. whom those present, as well as millions who watched on television, would remember longest. "When we let freedom ring," he cried, "when we let it ring from every village and every hamlet, from every state and every city, we will be able to speed up that day when all of God's children, black men and white men, Jews and Gentiles, Protestants and Catholics, will be able to join hands and sing, in the words of the old Negro* spiritual,

> Free at last,
> Free at last.
> Thank God Almighty,
> We are free at last."

King, now 34, was born at a time when blacks were considered inferior to whites—an attitude reinforced by laws segregating, or separating, them. There were separate schools, churches, even water fountains. He still recalls the curtains that were used in the dining cars of trains to separate whites from blacks. "I was very young when I had my first experience in sitting behind the curtain," he says. "I felt just as if a curtain had come down across my whole life. The insult of it I will never forget."

King and his teacher were once riding a bus from Macon to Atlanta when the driver ordered them to give up their seats to white passengers. "When we didn't move right away, the driver started cursing us out. I decided not to move at all, but my teacher pointed out that we must obey the law. So, we got up and stood in the aisle the whole 90 miles to Atlanta. It was a night I'll never forget. I don't think I have ever been so deeply angry in my life."

* This term was used to describe African Americans at the time this article was written.

Martin Luther King Jr.

Key Dates

1929 — Born in Atlanta on January 15

1957 — Founds Southern Christian Leadership Conference, an organization that advocates nonviolent struggle against racism

1963 — Delivers "I Have a Dream" speech at March on Washington supporting proposed civil rights legislation

1964 — Wins Nobel Peace Prize

1968 — Assassinated in Memphis

1983 — Birthday declared a national holiday

Focus: Reading for Understanding

1. What are civil-rights leaders? Who did Martin Luther King Jr. picture being "free at last"? Free from what?

2. How did King's boyhood experiences of discrimination affect him?

3. Why might King have decided not to move when asked to do so by the bus driver? Why did his teacher say they had to?

4. Examine the cover. What does it mean to "cast a long shadow"?

5. Word Watch—Look up the following words and note how they are used in the article: *spectacle, monument, hamlet, spiritual, inferior,* and *reinforced.*

Connect

Have you or has someone you know experienced discrimination? Discuss in pairs or small groups. Then, write a paragraph defining discrimination and describing your experience.

Explore

1. When King's teacher said they had to obey the law, the teacher was referring to what are known as "Jim Crow" laws. What were these laws?

2. The March on Washington, King's "I Have a Dream" speech, and the Birmingham protests were key events in the civil rights struggle. Find out more about them.

Nelson Mandela

Nelson Mandela
He helped dismantle apartheid in South Africa.

May 9, 1994

Just a short stroll from Nelson Mandela's modest country house in the Transkei is the even more humble village where he was born. The round thatched huts of Qunu have no running water or electricity, and shy herdboys carrying sticks tend the skinny cattle the same way young Rolihlahla Nelson Mandela did almost 70 years ago. Walking across the green hills above the village one morning not long ago, Mandela recalled a lesson he learned as a boy. "When you want to get a herd to move in a certain direction," he said, "you stand at the back with a stick. Then, a few of the more energetic cattle move to the front and the rest of the cattle follow. You are really guiding them from behind." He paused before saying with a smile, "That is how a leader should do his work."

No one would suggest that so charismatic a figure as Nelson Mandela, now 75, leads from behind. But Mandela has always made his authority felt on two levels: by standing at the head of the African National Congress, and by forming strategy from behind. During his career as a politician, he has at times moved ahead of his colleagues and boldly created policy. While at other times he has been content to plant the seed of an idea that bears fruit many years later.

Next week, Mandela will become the president of the country whose government he fought against for so long. Leading a liberation struggle is a task fundamentally different from heading a government; Mandela will no longer seek to bring a system down but to build one up. Yet his style of leadership is suited to his new task, for he is a seeker of unity and consensus.

To black audiences, he declares that democracy and majority rule will not change the circumstances of their lives overnight. At the same time, he informs white audiences that they must take responsibility for the past—in which South Africa was governed under a system of apartheid, or strict racial segregation. He adds that they will have to adjust to a future of majority rule.

As president of South Africa, he will no longer seek to bring a system down but to build one up.

Mandela does not always get his way. During his imprisonment on Robben Island, he wanted to stage a strike to force the warders to address prisoners with the word "Mr." But, he was always turned down by his comrades. Last year he urged the ANC to reduce the voting age to 14, but his colleagues refused. Once he has lost, he publicly speaks in favor of the position he opposed. "I sometimes come to the National Executive Committee with an idea and they overrule me," he recently observed. "And I obey them, even when they are wrong," he added with a smile. "That is democracy."

Nelson Mandela

Key Dates

1918 — Born in the Transkei on July 18

1944 — Joins the African National Congress (ANC), dedicated to ending apartheid in South Africa

1962–1990 — Imprisoned because he advocated sabotage

1991 — Becomes president of the ANC

1993 — Shares the Nobel Peace Prize with F.W. de Klerk for dismantling apartheid

1994–1998 — Serves as South Africa's president

Focus: Reading for Understanding

1. What is Nelson Mandela's philosophy of leadership? Where did his ideas come from?

2. What position did Mandela assume in 1994? What had he been doing before this?

3. What was Mandela's goal as president, for both white and black South Africans?

4. What is *apartheid*?

5. Word Watch—Look up the following words and note how they are used in the article: *modest, humble, charismatic, authority, colleagues, boldly, content, liberation, unity, consensus, majority, segregation, strike, warders, comrades, urged, reduce, colleagues, opposed,* and *overrule.*

Connect

What is your idea of good leadership? Make a list of qualities you think a leader needs.

Explore

1. Where is South Africa? What is the country known for, both politically and in terms of tourism and natural resources?

2. Find out more about the history and accomplishments of the ANC. Who is its leader today?

Mao Zedong

TWENTY CENTS

TIME

THE WEEKLY NEWSMAGAZINE

民主統一

CHINA'S MAO TSE-TUNG
The Communist Boss learned tyranny as a boy.

$6.00 A YEAR

Mao Zedong

He brought Communism to China.

February 7, 1949

Thirty-seven years ago, in the Hunan Provincial Library at Changsha, a 19-year-old farm lad looked at a map of the world for the first time in his narrow life. He studied it, as he later recalled, with great interest. Last week, the farm lad was redrawing that map with an iron pen dipped in blood. Mao Zedong was adding China to the domain of world Communism.

> ## "Whoever dares to turn in the opposite direction will...get his head broken against the wall."

For the West, the event was a major disaster, still incalculable in its consequences. For Communism, it was the greatest victory since the Russian Revolution. For most of the Chinese people, it meant peace—but only in the sense that large-scale fighting would stop. It also meant the kind of war that the Chinese have often known: the silent, constant war that tyrannical governments wage upon their people.

For Mao Zedong, the peasant lad, the event had enormous meaning. He was about to be master over the vast land that had bred him, over the cities and libraries, over half a billion tough, tired people who listened last week as the Communist faithful sang Mao's glory.

What kind of master will Mao be to China? In a pamphlet entitled "The New Democracy," Mao carefully explained how he intends to rule China. Land must be "equalized" and capital "controlled." Warns Mao: "Whoever dares to turn in the opposite direction will . . . get his head broken against the wall . . . Raise your fists, new China will be ours!"

Mao may have to break many a Chinese head in trying to rule China, probably the biggest task ever taken on by Communism. As he has put it, "A revolution is no invitation to a banquet."

The Chinese people have tolerated many conquerors. But the one who prepared to take over China last week could rival all of them. Once, while flying over a civil war battlefield on which his men fought, Mao wrote a poem:

In clear weather

The earth is so charming.

Like a red-faced girl clothed in white.

Such is the charm of these rivers and mountains

Calling innumerable heroes to vie with each other in pursuing her.

The emperors Shih Huang and Wu Ti were barely cultured,

The emperors Tai Tsung and Tai Tsu were lacking in feeling,

Genghis Khan knew only how to bend his bow at the eagles,

These all belong to the past—only today are there men of feeling.

Mao is a man of feeling, all right, but as tough and tyrannical as any emperor who had preceded him in the rule of his great and long-suffering land.

Mao Zedong

Key Dates

1893 — Born in Hunan province on December 26

1949 — Proclaims the People's Republic of China and becomes its first leader, intent on turning China into a socialist state modeled on the Soviet Union. Most China scholars agree that at least one million people were executed over the next six years.

1966 — Begins the Cultural Revolution

1972 — Meets Richard Nixon in Beijing

1976 — Dies of a heart attack

Focus: Reading for Understanding

1. What did Mao Zedong's takeover of China mean to the Western world?

2. In "The New Democracy," how did Mao say he intended to rule China? From this brief article, does it sound like Mao ran a democracy as we know it in the United States?

3. In his poem, Mao reviews the leaders of China before him and finds them all inferior to himself, a "man of feeling." But how does the author claim Mao compares to them?

4. Word Watch—Look up the following words and note how they are used in the article: *domain, incalculable, consequences, tyrannical, bred, equalized, capital, tolerated, conqueror, innumerable, pursuing, cultured,* and *preceded.*

Connect

Read about President Richard Nixon and his role with China. What was significant about Nixon's 1972 visit to China?

Explore

1. Find out how Mao came to power in China and what happened during his rule.

2. What happened when university students protested in Beijing's Tiananmen Square in 1989?

Thurgood Marshall

TWENTY CENTS   SEPTEMBER 19, 1955

TIME

THE WEEKLY NEWSMAGAZINE

THURGOOD
MARSHALL

$6.00 A YEAR   VOL. LXVI NO. 12

Thurgood Marshall

He fought to end school segregation.

September 19, 1955

As the nation's children trooped back to school in September of 1955, one of the most important changes on the U.S. scene was the astounding progress of racial desegregation. In Kansas City and Oklahoma City, in Oak Ridge and Charleston, white and Negro* children for the first time sat together in classrooms. This simple fact resulted from a legal victory: the U.S. Supreme Court's decisions of May 17, 1954, and May 31, 1955, holding segregated schools contrary to the Fourteenth Amendment.

> ## "This court should make it clear that [segregation] is not what our Constitution stands for."

The name on this victory is that of Thurgood Marshall, 47, a constitutional lawyer for the National Association for the Advancement of Colored* People. He is at his sincerest in declaring that he is only one of the millions, white and Negro, whose courage, sweat, skill, imagination, and common sense made the victory possible.

In presenting his case before the Supreme Court, Marshall managed to get into a few strong sentences his analysis of the South's attitude: "I got the feeling on hearing the discussion yesterday," he said, "that when you put a white child in a school with a whole lot of colored children, the child would fall apart or something. Everybody knows that is not true. Those same kids in Virginia and South Carolina—and I have seen them do it—they play in the streets together, they play on their farms, they separate to go to school, they come out of school and play ball together. They have to be separated in school. Why, of all the groups of people in this country, [do] you have to single out the Negroes and give them this separate treatment? It can't be because of slavery in the past, because there are very few groups in this country that haven't had slavery some place back in the history of their groups. It can't be color, because there are Negroes as white as the drifted snow, with blue eyes, and they are just as segregated as the colored men. The only thing it can be is a determination that the people who were formerly in slavery shall be kept as near that stage as is possible. And now is the time that this court should make it clear that that is not what our Constitution stands for."

This, and Marshall's social-scientist approach, paid off. In his opinion for the whole court, Chief Justice Earl Warren in sentence after sentence reflected the conviction that under present conditions of U.S. life, education could not be separate and equal. When he heard the decision read, Marshall said, "I was so happy, I was numb."

* This term was used to describe African Americans at the time this article was written.

Thurgood Marshall

Key Dates

1908 — Born in Baltimore, Maryland, on July 2

1938 — Becomes legal director of the national NAACP

1954 — Wins landmark ruling in *Brown v. Board of Education* when Supreme Court declares "separate but equal" public schools violate the Constitution

1967 — Appointed to the Supreme Court by President Lyndon Johnson

1993 — Dies on January 24

Focus: Reading for Understanding

1. What is racial segregation? What is desegregation? Why were schools segregated in America before 1954?

2. What arguments did Thurgood Marshall make to the Supreme Court? What was his "legal victory"? What did Supreme Court Justice Earl Warren mean when he ruled that public schools could not be "separate but equal"?

3. In what ways did America's classrooms change following the Supreme Court's *Brown v. Board of Education* decision?

4. Word Watch—Look up these words and note how they are used in the article: *segregation, desegregation, contrary, social scientist,* and *conviction.*

Connect

1. Read what Marshall told the Supreme Court. Then, explain what he said in your own words.

2. How diverse is your school and/or community?

Explore

1. Look up the Fourteenth Amendment to the Constitution. What does it mean that segregated schools were contrary to the Fourteenth Amendment?

2. Pretend that you are a lawyer arguing *Brown v. Board of Education* before the Supreme Court. Write your own argument. Then, present it to your class.

Golda Meir

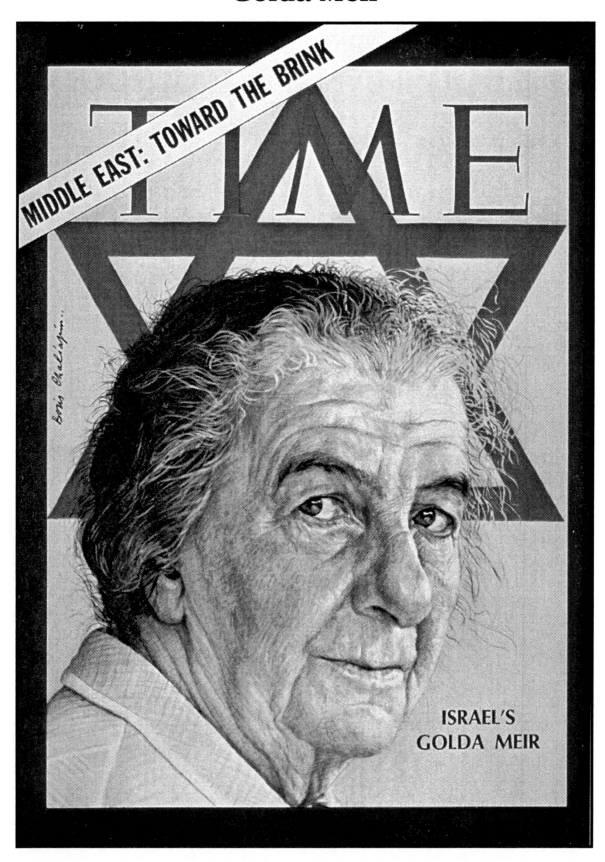

MIDDLE EAST: TOWARD THE BRINK

TIME

ISRAEL'S
GOLDA MEIR

Golda Meir
She led Israel with a firm hand.

September 19, 1969

For a few suspenseful days last week, the telephone wires hummed between Israel's general staff and a grandmotherly looking woman who is the country's premier. Golda Meir, 71, listened to reports of clashes between Israeli and Egyptian military units. At week's end, in a message marking Rosh Hashanah, the Jewish New Year, she ushered in the year 5730 on the Hebrew calendar with a warning to the Arab nations. "Attacks on the frontiers, sabotage attempts within Israel and attacks of piracy against Israelis abroad," she said, "have fortified Israel's resolve never to return to the situation of constant peril which prevailed before the Six-Day War." They were tough words from a tough lady. Golda Meir became premier six months ago, after the death of Levi Eshkol. She inherited the difficult task of overseeing the territories captured during the Six-Day War: the Sinai Peninsula, the Gaza Strip, the West Bank of the Jordan River, and the Golan Heights. Says Meir: "I don't know when peace will come. But I have no doubt that it will."

Golda Meir's character, like that of the state of Israel, was shaped in the ghettos of Europe and drew on a heritage of two millennia of sorrow and insecurity. The essence of the woman is conviction, without compromise. She seldom loses an argument.

Like many other Israelis of her generation, Mrs. Meir was born in Russia. At the age of eight, she emigrated from Pinsk to Milwaukee. She can still recall the early days in Russia, when her family regularly boarded up the windows as protection against gangs bent on pogroms against the Jewish people. On one occasion, while she was playing in the streets with other Jewish children, cossacks spurred their horses to jump over the heads of the children. "If there is any logical explanation for the direction that my life has taken," she said many years later, "it is the desire and determination to save Jewish children from a similar scene and from a similar experience."

"I don't know when peace will come. But I have no doubt that it will."

Meir later married, moved to Jerusalem and tried to concentrate on raising her son and daughter. As the Jews pressed toward independence for their state, she was sent to the United States to raise money for weapons. In less than three months she collected $50 million, and David Ben-Gurion referred to her as "the Jewish woman who got the money that made the state possible." On the eve of Israel's nationhood, she went to Amman to see Jordan's King Abdullah. Dressed as an Arab woman, she secretly crossed the Arab lines. Abdullah asked her to delay proclaiming the state. She replied: "We have been waiting for 2,000 years. Is that hurrying?"

Golda Meir

Key Dates

1898 — Born in Kiev, Russia, on May 3

1906 — Moves with her family to Milwaukee, Wisconsin

1921 — Emigrates to Palestine

1948 — Israel becomes a state

1949– 1956 — Serves as Israel's minister of labor

1966 — Becomes prime minister

1973 — Leads Israel during war with Egypt

1974 — Resigns from office

1978 — Dies in Jerusalem

Focus: Reading for Understanding

1. What warning did Golda Meir give to the Arab nations in 1969?

2. What challenges did Meir inherit as Israel's premier?

3. How did Meir's childhood experiences affect her future? Why would saving Jewish children be a "logical explanation" of her past?

4. Why would the artist include a blue star behind Meir on the cover?

5. Word Watch—Look up the following words and note how they are used in the article: *premier, ushered, frontiers, sabotage, piracy, fortified, resolve, prevailed, ghettos, emigrated, pogroms,* and *cossacks.*

Connect

1. Find stories in a national newspaper about the continuing struggle for peace in the Middle East. What is happening in the region today?

2. Pretend you are Meir. Describe in a journal entry your secret journey to see King Abdullah.

Explore

1. When and why was the state of Israel established?

2. On a map of the Middle East, locate all the places in the article.

3. Find out more about the Six-Day War, David Ben-Gurion, and King Abdullah of Jordan.

Maria Montessori

TIME
The Weekly Newsmagazine

Volume XV

DOTTORESSA MARIA MONTESSORI
Translation cost: one guinea.
(See EDUCATION)

Number 5

Maria Montessori

A famous teacher returns to her homeland.

February 3, 1930

Last week in Rome, a woman stood up to receive the applause of learned contemporaries and the acclaim of one hundred followers from twenty-one nations. Dottoressa (Doctor) Maria Montessori had come home to conduct her own new experimental school—the Opera Montessori—after sixteen years of lecturing abroad.

When women weren't supposed to have minds of their own, she devoted her life to studying the minds of children.

Some distance from the Opera Montessori is a place where, in the last decade of the nineteenth century, a young woman medical student was made fun of by male classmates. Women were not then supposed to have technical careers, or minds of their own, or the liberty of going about the city unchaperoned. But Maria Montessori had the satisfaction of being the first woman to get an M.D. from the University of Rome.

Her degree got her a position on the staff of a city clinic. Through patient experimentation, she discovered that if children were given something to twist and touch with their hands, their brains might learn to respond.

In 1898, she became director of a state school. Here was formulated the nucleus of what most educators now know as the Montessori Plan, a system for teaching young children.

The Montessori Plan took root early in the United States. Anne George, a graduate of a 1911 Montessori training course, went to Washington to further the Montessori cause. There she met Mrs. Alexander Graham Bell with whom she founded the Montessori Educational Association. Among famed United States children who have been educated under the Montessori methods are the grandchildren of Alexander Graham Bell and the actor Douglas Fairbanks Jr.

Most United States educators point out that the educator John Dewey also emphasized the importance of connecting the infant's use of its hands and its brain. The system that came from Dewey's philosophy differs from the Montessori Plan. Under the Dewey method, the child has an opportunity for creative expression which the less flexible Montessori method does not allow.

Maria Montessori

Key Dates

1870 — Born on August 31 in Chiarevalle

1896 — Becomes Italy's first female physician

1903 — Teaches anthropology in Rome, Italy

1906 — Founds Casa dei Bambini (children's school) in Italy

1919 — Begins teacher training courses in London

1929 — Founds the Association Montessori Internationale in Amsterdam

1949–1951 — Nominated for the Nobel Peace Prize three years in a row

1952 — Dies in the Netherlands

Focus: Reading for Understanding

1. At which university did Maria Montessori become the first woman to receive an M.D.?

2. What did Montessori discover about children while working as a physician?

3. What other educator has also emphasized the importance of the connection between the hand and the brain?

4. Word Watch—Look up the following words and note how they are used in the article: *contemporaries, acclaim, differs, philosophy, nucleus, liberty, formulated, unchaperoned,* and *famed.*

Connect

Montessori was a leader in education, but also showed the world that women are capable. Find out about Oprah Winfrey. What contributions has she made for children's well being?

Explore

1. Montessori was nominated for the Nobel Peace Prize three years in a row. What is the Nobel Peace Prize? Research this and report your findings to the class. Who are some individuals that have won this prize through the years?

2. If possible, visit a Montessori school in your area. How is it different from a traditional school? What makes it unique?

Mother Teresa

Mother Teresa

She brought love and hope to India's poor.

December 29, 1975

The starving and the dying seem to be concentrated in Calcutta as nowhere else in India—or the world. Their numbers grow daily. At least 200,000 of them live in the streets, building tiny fires to cook their scraps of food, curling up in their cotton rags against a wall to sleep—and often to die. Out of this scene has come an extraordinary message of love and hope. Its bearer is a tiny gray-eyed Roman Catholic nun who 27 years ago, alone and penniless, set out to work among the city's "poorest of the poor."

Today, Mother Teresa of Calcutta, 65, is slightly bent from hardship, her man-size hands are gnarled, her Albanian peasant face is seamed. From her solitary, seemingly foolhardy labors have grown two orders of women and men willing to take risks and make sacrifices. Nearly 1,300 Missionaries of Charity—1,132 nuns and 150 brothers—are now scattered throughout 67 countries tending the world's poor: in Yemen and Gaza, in Australia and Peru, in London and in New York City's South Bronx—even, at Pope Paul VI's request, in the shadow of St. Peter's.

Calcutta is still the heart of the effort. There, Mother Teresa and her followers collect the dying from the streets so that they may leave life in peace among friends. They rescue abandoned newborn babies from garbage heaps. They nurse them back to health if they can and find homes for them later. They seek out the diseased and the hurt. They have made havens for lepers, the retarded, and the mad. They have found work for the jobless.

"The poor are our brothers and sisters."

Between her travels to the order's various outposts, Mother Teresa rises at 4:30 A.M., prays, sings the Mass with her sister nuns, joins them for a meal of an egg, bread, banana, and tea, then goes out into the city to work. Age and authority have not changed her; she is at ease these days with pope and prime minister, but she still cleans convent toilets. "The poor are our brothers and sisters," she says. "There are people in the world who need love, who need care, who have to be wanted." Mother Teresa's own loving spirit prompts many to bestow on her a title that she would surely reject. She is, they say, a living saint.

Perhaps the best definition of sainthood is one that draws remarkable agreement: the saint as a window through which another world is glimpsed, a person through whom the light of God shines. It is just that light that many see in Mother Teresa.

Mother Teresa

Key Dates

1910 — Born in Shkup, Ottoman Empire, on August 27

1928 — Joins Irish convent

1929 — Sent to Darjeeling, India

1931 — Begins teaching at a Calcutta girls' school

1946 — Receives "call" to live and work among the poor

1963 — Receives India's Padmashri humanitarian award

1979 — Wins Nobel Peace Prize

1997 — Dies in Calcutta

Focus: Reading for Understanding

1. Why was Mother Teresa considered a "living saint"? How did her calling to help the poor inspire others around the world?

2. How is street life in Calcutta described?

3. Word Watch—Look up the following words and note how they are used in the article: *concentrated, hardship, gnarled, foolhardy, labors, orders, missionaries, havens, lepers, outposts, prompts,* and *bestow.*

Connect

1. Explain Mother Teresa's philosophy in your own words. Do you share her beliefs? Discuss in pairs or groups.

2. Do you or does anyone you know participate in volunteer or charity work, perhaps through a religious or community organization? Write about your experience.

3. "Think globally, act locally." How does this idea relate to Mother Teresa's work?

Explore

1. Locate Calcutta on a map. What factors contribute to the problem of poverty in India?

2. What resources are available in your community to help people in need? What resources are available to help people around the world in need (for example, UNICEF)?

3. Why did Mother Teresa win the Nobel Peace Prize? Who else has won it?

Richard Nixon

Richard Nixon
He built a bridge to China.

July 26, 1971

"It was a very moving occasion. It is not often one can say he has participated in turning a new page in history."—Henry Kissinger

In just 90 seconds of television time last week, President Richard Nixon made an announcement that altered many of the major assumptions and patterns of postwar diplomacy. The president would go to Peking to meet with China's Mao Zedong and Premier Chou En-lai before next May. His National Security Adviser, Henry Kissinger, had made the arrangements during a secret meeting with Chou in Peking the week before.

"The aim of the meeting," said the president, "is to seek the normalization of relations between the two countries and also to exchange views on questions of concern to the two sides." The statement brought an instant response. "This is a turning point in world history—I cannot remember anything in my lifetime more exciting or more encouraging," declared England's Lord Caradon, former ambassador to the United Nations.

Nixon will become the first Western head of state to visit Peking since Mao's revolutionaries drove Chiang Kai-shek's government out of power and instituted Communism in 1949. The president will thus dramatically shatter nearly a quarter-century of total official silence between the two powers. The announcement of a summit meeting throws relationships among many nations, large and small, into dramatic new perspectives.

Far more personally, the U.S. president stands a chance to emerge as a peacemaker in time for a needed boost in popularity before he faces a tough reelection campaign in the fall of 1972. It would be ironic—and yet appropriate—if the man who launched his political career largely on the basis of his opposition to Communism were to cap it by establishing himself as a leader who helped move the capitalist and Communist worlds toward a historic dialogue.

Nixon shattered nearly a quarter-century of total official silence between China and the United States.

Nixon explained his motives in a recent meeting with newspaper editors. China, he argued, will one day be "an enormous economic power," and its continued isolation from international affairs must be ended before it becomes a threat to peace. Nixon looked 15 or 20 years into the future and observed: "Mainland China, outside the world community, completely isolated, with its leaders not in communication with world leaders, would be a danger to the whole world that would be unacceptable to us and unacceptable to others as well."

Richard Nixon

Key Dates

1913 — Born on January 9 in Yorba Linda, California

1946–1950 — U.S. representative from California

1950–1952 — U.S. senator

1952–1960 — Vice president of the United States

1962 — Defeated in California governor race

1968–1974 — President of the United States

1972 — Visits China

1974 — Resigns presidency on August 9 as a result of the Watergate scandal

1994 — Dies on April 22 in New York

Focus: Reading for Understanding

1. What was so historic about President Richard Nixon's announcement that he would go to China?

2. What was the goal of Nixon's trip?

3. What did Nixon stand to gain personally from this trip?

4. Looking into the future, what did Nixon see as the threat from mainland China?

5. Word Watch—Look up the following words and note how they are used in the article: *altered, assumptions, postwar, diplomacy, normalization, former, revolutionaries, dramatically, shatter, summit, emerge, boost, motives,* and *isolation.*

Connect

1. Find out about Gerald Ford. What role did Gerald Ford play in Nixon's presidency? How is he related to this profile on Nixon?

Explore

1. Find Peking (Beijing) and mainland China on a world map. What is the current population of China? Of the United States?

2. Since Nixon's visit, what has been the relationship between the United States and China? What recent events have strained the relationship?

3. Why did Nixon resign as president in 1974?

Kwame Nkrumah

TWENTY CENTS

GOLD COAST'S KWAME NKRUMAH
In the Dark Continent, dawn's early light?

$6.00 A YEAR

Kwame Nkrumah

Sunrise on the Gold Coast

February 9, 1953

Through the streets of Accra, capital of the Gold Coast, democracy ran joyously wild. The women in the parade were slim and graceful, furled like striped umbrellas into acres of colorful cotton cloth. The men wore shirts open at the neck which hung outside their shorts. Everyone in the procession was black and proud of it.

Suddenly, the noisy crowd parted. Through a forest of waving palm branches, an open car bore a husky black man with fine sculptured lips, melancholy eyes, and a halo of frizzy black hair. The Right Honorable Kwame Nkrumah (En-kroom-ah), prime minister of the Gold Coast, waved a white handkerchief to his people as they sought to touch the hem of his tunic.

Nkrumah's 4.5 million countrymen speak a range of languages and are scattered across a rectangular patch of jungle, swamp, and bushland. Seven out of ten are illiterate, more than half believe in witchcraft, yet the happy-go-lucky Gold Coasters have been chosen by imperial Britain to pioneer its boldest experiment in African home rule. In 1951, the British gave the Gold Coast its first democratic constitution. Last year they designated Kwame Nkrumah as prime minister.

Nkrumah was born in the mud-hut village of Nkroful where his father hammered out gold ornaments for local woodcutters. Nkrumah studied at a Catholic mission school and a Gold Coast college. Then, a generous uncle paid his way to the United States. He spent eight years at Lincoln University in Pennsylvania, where he earned three degrees.

From there he went to England to take a law degree at London University.

Nkrumah wanted more. He demanded "self-government NOW."

While he was in London, the cause of African nationalism was heating up at home. Nkrumah was picked to head the United Gold Coast Convention (UGCC), which was demanding home rule. Soon, the British were presented with a new constitution that called for popular elections. The UGCC's slogan had been "self-government in our time." Nkrumah wanted more. He demanded "self-government NOW." He formed the Convention People's Party (CPP).

Last March, the British government approved Kwame Nkrumah as full prime minister. Now, he feels the full responsibility of leading his people to complete self-government. Of the Gold Coasters, he says, "They must not make me go too fast—and I must not go too slow. If I tried to stop their urge to be free, they would turn on me. My job is to keep things level and steady."

It is in the jubilant Gold Coast, and in its hero Nkrumah, that some of Africa's awakening millions see the early light of freedom dawning over the continent.

Kwame Nkrumah

Key Dates

1909 — Born in Nkroful, Ghana

1948–1951 — Forms political party; jailed by Britain (Ghana's ruler)

1950s — Leads country's drive for independence

1951 — Released from jail to become prime minister of Gold Coast (now Ghana)

1957 — Ghana becomes the first African nation to win independence from Britain

1960 — Elected president of Ghana

1966 — Ousted from office

1972 — Dies in exile

Focus: Reading for Understanding

1. Seven out of ten people in the Gold Coast were illiterate at the time of the article. Where was Kwame Nkrumah educated?

2. What was the CPP? How was it formed?

3. Why was this self-government in the Gold Coast called an experiment?

4. Word Watch—Look up the following words and note how they are used in the article: *slogan, witchcraft, melancholy, procession, jubilant, illiterate, designated,* and *self-government.*

Connect

What qualities does Nkrumah have that made him a good leader? What qualities does a leader need?

Explore

1. Research other leaders such as Nelson Mandela and Martin Luther King Jr. How are these leaders similar and different compared to Nkrumah?

2. What is self-government? Research to find out the role Britain plays in African countries today.

Sandra Day O'Connor

JULY 20, 1981 $1.50

TIME

Justice—At Last

STREETS OF ANGER
Why Britain Burns

Reagan Nominee
Sandra O'Connor

Sandra Day O'Connor

The Supreme Court's first female justice

July 20, 1981

Ronald Reagan lived up to a campaign pledge last week, and the nation cheered. At a hastily arranged television appearance in the White House press room, the president referred to his promise as a candidate that he would name a woman to the Supreme Court. He explained: "That is not to say I would appoint a woman merely to do so. That would not be fair to women, nor to future generations of all Americans whose lives are so deeply affected by decisions of the court. Rather, I pledged to appoint a woman who meets the very high standards I demand of all court appointees." So saying, he introduced his nominee to succeed retiring Associate Justice Potter Stewart as "a person for all seasons," with "unique qualities of temperament, fairness, intellectual capacity." She was Sandra Day O'Connor, 51, the first woman to serve as majority leader of a U.S. state legislature and, since 1979, a judge in the Arizona State Court of Appeals.

O'Connor's name had been floated about in rumors ever since Stewart, 66, announced his intention to retire last month, but her nomination, which must be approved by the senate in September, was a stunning break with tradition. In its 191-year history, 101 judges have served on the nation's highest court, and all have been men. By giving the brethren their first sister, Reagan provided not only a breakthrough on the bench but a powerful push forward in the shamefully long and needlessly tortuous march of women toward full equality in American society.

The president had the imagination and good sense to break down a useless barrier by naming a woman to the Supreme Court.

In presenting Sandra O'Connor to the press, Reagan described his right to nominate Supreme Court justices as the presidency's "most awesome appointment" power. What is important is that he had the imagination and good sense to break down a useless discriminatory barrier by naming a woman to the nation's Supreme Court—at last. America waits to see what place in legal history will be carved out by this daunting daughter of Arizona pioneers.

Patricia Ireland, a Miami attorney and regional director of the National Organization for Women, said she was "thrilled and excited" by the selection, adding: "Nine older men do not have the same perspective on issues like sex discrimination, reproductive rights or the issues that affect women directly." Declared former Texas Congresswoman Barbara Jordan, a lawyer, "I congratulate the president."

Sandra Day O'Connor

Key Dates

1930 — Born in El Paso, Texas, on March 26

1965–1969 — Serves as assistant attorney general in Arizona

1969–1974 — Elected to Arizona state senate

1974 — Appointed Arizona state judge

1979 — Named to Arizona Court of Appeals

1981 — Becomes first female justice of the U.S. Supreme Court

2006 — Resigns from the Supreme Court on January 31; currently serves as Chancellor of the College of William and Mary

Focus: Reading for Understanding

1. What campaign promise concerning the U.S. Supreme Court did Ronald Reagan make? Under what circumstances did he honor his promise? How did the nation react?

2. Explain the historical importance of this "stunning break with tradition." What standards did Sandra Day O'Connor have to meet? What was her background? How did President Reagan describe her?

3. Word Watch—Look up the following words and note how they are used in the article: *candidate, appoint, nominee, temperament, intellectual, majority, retire, brethren, tortuous, discriminatory, daunting,* and *reproductive.*

Connect

1. Can you name other people who have been "firsts" in any field? Have you been a "first" in your family, class, school, or community? What are the challenges and privileges of being a "first"? Share your ideas and experiences.

2. Does gender matter in how well someone can do a job? Discuss.

Explore

1. Research the role of the Supreme Court in the United States. Name all nine current justices.

2. Learn more about Ruth Bader Ginsburg, another female Supreme Court Justice.

Eva Perón

TWENTY CENTS

TIME

THE WEEKLY NEWSMAGAZINE

EVA PERÓN
Between two worlds, an Argentine rainbow.

Boris Chaliapin

$6.00 A YEAR

Eva Perón

She made headlines at home and abroad.

July 14, 1947

As a First Lady, there had never been anything in Argentina like Eva Perón. Just as her husband, President Juan Perón, had risen to power by playing expertly on the feelings of Argentina's unhappy workers, so Eva made women's liberation her battle cry. She was the new woman, free and unchained.

With great fervor, she encouraged the public to call her "Evita" in a land where nicknames are used by only the closest friends. Huge, larger-than-life pictures of the first lady blossomed all over the country with the legend: "I prefer to be simply Evita to being the wife of the president, if this Evita is used to better conditions in the homes of my country."

Devoted and well aware of his wife's value as a press agent, Juan gave her a free hand with her campaign for women's suffrage, her labor reforms, and her many charities. Eva still has no official title, but every day she shows up in her office to work from 9:00 A.M. to noon receiving workers and trade unionists, hearing hard-luck stories, and giving advice and aid. In the afternoons, Eva is on her rounds again, visiting factories, addressing workers, or distributing money to the needy.

In the first 11 months of their joint reign, Eva has given away in her husband's name some $4,280,000 worth of schoolbooks, clothes, shoes, furniture, toys, cakes, and cider. The gifts are always accompanied by one of Eva's flowery speeches, with constant reference to the "heart of Perón" and the "heart of Evita."

> **...she encouraged the public to call her "Evita" in a land where nicknames are used by only the closest friends.**

In Argentina, Eva holds the official title of "First Samaritan," but whether her unbounded love for the masses has been repaid in kind is open to question. Eva has few close friends and many enemies. She constantly interferes in state affairs, and it is certain that her palace intrigues have earned her husband many an enemy he might not otherwise have had. Yet Eva, her waxen face as deadpan as it always is when she is not smiling, will insist time and again that her husband governs alone, neither asking nor getting her advice. "I am his wife," she says, "and I am interested only in social work."

Eva Perón

Key Dates

1919 — Born on May 7

1935–1943 — Works in nightclubs and at the theater in Buenos Aries; career advances to radio and films; meets Colonel Juan Perón

1945 — Eva and Juan are married on October 21

1946 — Juan Perón is elected president

1947 — Represents Argentina on a goodwill tour of Europe; her visit receives worldwide coverage

1952 — Makes her last public appearance at her husband's inauguration ceremony on June 4; dies on July 26

Focus: Reading for Understanding

1. Juan Perón became president by playing on the feelings of unhappy workers. Who did Eva Perón "liberate"?

2. What issues was Perón interested in? What did the words "free and unchained" mean in relation to the Argentine women?

3. Perón held what official title in Argentina?

4. Word Watch—Look up the following words and note how they are used in the article: *liberation, fervor, unionists, waxen, suffrage, intrigues, press agent,* and *interferes.*

Connect

1. Explain Perón's beliefs in your own words. Do you share her beliefs? Discuss in small groups.

2. What do you think is the role of a leader's wife? Explain your views as a class.

Explore

1. Who is First Lady of Argentina today? Using research, find out what the people in Argentina think of this lady.

2. Research to find out more about Evita. How did she die? Why does she still hold the heart of Argentina?

3. Perón was a very charismatic person. Look up the word "charismatic," and make a list of famous people you think are charismatic

Ronald Reagan

Ronald Reagan

A skilled communicator with small-town roots

July 7, 1986

In an interview in the Oval Office last week with TIME's White House correspondents, President Reagan gave glimpses into his character and popularity by reminiscing about events that helped shape his outlook.

"Maybe it goes back to a small-town beginning in which you were aware of how people rallied around whenever there was a need," replied the native of Tampico, Illinois, when asked if he felt a special relationship with the American people. "And then, another plus that I would repeat if I had to do it over again: I went to a quite small college, and in a small college there is no way you can be anonymous… I don't think even *like* is enough of a word. I *love* people."

Reagan bristles at the notion that he is not popular among the nation's poor and among those who think his policies are harsh. It is only "propaganda," he insists, that his budgets have cut heavily into federal programs for nutrition and hunger. "We were poor when I was young, but the difference then was the government didn't come around telling you you were poor," he says, harking back to the tradition of community help from sources other than the government. "My mother, God rest her soul, was the kindest, God-loving person I have ever known. She was always finding some family or someone that needed help and that we could help, and yet we were poor… I think back on all the places along the line where somebody stepped out of line and helped—and it's always been that way—the people that lent a hand at the time when you needed a hand."

> **"We were poor when I was young, but the difference then was the government didn't come around telling you you were poor."**

"I believe in taking the big issues to the people," he says, paraphrasing Thomas Jefferson's belief that the "American people, if they know all the facts, will never make a mistake." It was a talent he learned in an earlier career as an actor. "The very soul of show business is communicating."

One secret to Reagan's appeal, which is also the source of much criticism, is that he relates far more easily to the plight of individual citizens than to social problems in the abstract. As an actor in Hollywood, he was shown a letter from a girl who said she was dying and wanted an autographed picture. Reagan at first refused, saying the letter was probably phony, but his father talked him into it. "Two weeks later I received a letter from a nurse in the hospital that told me that the girl who'd written had died holding my picture in her hands." It taught him a "lifetime lesson," Reagan recalls, "that never again will I feel that impatient or come that close to saying no to anyone."

Ronald Reagan

Key Dates

1911 — Born in Tampico, Illinois, on February 6

1947 — Elected president of the Screen Actors Guild

1952 — Marries Nancy Davis

1962 — Changes from Democrat to Republican

1966 — Elected California's governor (reelected in 1970)

1980 — Defeats Jimmy Carter to become U.S. president

1981 — Shot in assassination attempt

1884 — Reelected president

2004 — Dies on June 5

Focus: Reading for Understanding

1. What factors in his background most influenced Ronald Reagan?

2. How did Reagan's training as an actor help him as a politician?

3. What was the "lifetime lesson" that Reagan learned from the hospital story?

4. After reading the article, answer the question on the cover: "Why is this man so popular?"

5. Word Watch—Look up the following words and note how they are used in the article: *reminiscing, rallied, anonymous, bristles, propaganda, harking back, communicator, paraphrasing,* and *plight.*

Connect

1. Read about other U.S. presidents. Carter was a peanut farmer and Reagan was an actor. Are there other presidents who took nontraditional routes to the presidency? Research a president not featured in this collection.

2. Are you a good communicator? What do you think makes for good communication? Brainstorm a list of criteria as a class.

Explore

Watch a video starring Reagan. What are your impressions of Reagan as a communicator?

Diego Rivera

TWENTY CENTS

TIME

THE WEEKLY NEWSMAGAZINE

DIEGO RIVERA (SELF-PORTRAIT)
Rotten duck is for educated noses.
(Art)

$6.00 A YEAR

Diego Rivera
He created art that his country could call its own.

April 4, 1949

In the center of Mexico City squats a vast edifice of white marble, imported block by block from Italy. It is the Palace of Fine Arts. Inside the museum's marble halls last week, workmen were uncrating the paintings of one Mexican who took Europe in his stride and came home to enrich his country with great art that it could call its own. His name: Diego Rivera. The crates in the Palace of Fine Arts held 500 pictures that were assembled for a show opening in May. The show would help clinch Rivera's reputation as the Western Hemisphere's finest living painter.

"…you can't express what you don't feel."

Diego Rivera was born sixty-two years ago in the mountain town of Guanajuato. Young Diego got into the San Carlos Academy of Fine Arts when he was only eleven, but his real teacher was José Posada, whose printmaking shop stood near the school. "I used to peer in his window every evening," says Rivera, "until at last he invited me inside. We talked together for seven years about politics and art. He taught me the connection between art and life; that you can't express what you don't feel." At age 20, Diego won a scholarship and spent the next years in Europe where he "gobbled up museums."

Full of the idea of painting "for the millions," Rivera hastened home from Paris in 1921 and joined forces with two other revolutionaries who were to make Mexican art history: Siqueiros and José Clemente Orozco. Together they formed a government-backed syndicate of artists. To syndicate meant ditching easel painting and going to work on walls—wherever they could find a big, challenging, bare one. In the next decade, Rivera did what is probably his greatest work: 124 frescoes in the Ministry of Education, a historical mural in the Cortés Palace in Cuernavaca, and his frescoes in the old chapel that had been part of the Agricultural School at Chapingo. Diego's murals heavily influenced the WPA (Works Progress Administration) muralists who spread their work across the walls of U.S. post offices in the 1930s.

For the past seven years, Rivera has been chipping away at a project close to his heart. He is building a monument to himself at the edge of a lava bed near Mexico City. Though it is only half finished, the monument already looks as ancient as something Hernán Cortés might have found in 1519. Rivera considers it more important than any of his paintings. "I have always wanted to do architecture, and this could be the beginning of a new architectural tradition in Mexico—part Aztec, part Mayan, and also my own."

Diego Rivera

Key Dates

1886 — Born in Guanajuato, Mexico

1896 — Begins evening art courses

1907 — Wins scholarship to study art in Spain

1907–1918 — Lives and studies in Spain, France, and Italy

1913 — Begins painting in the cubist style

1920s — Visits the Soviet Union

1932–1933 — Paints murals for the Detroit Institute of Arts and the RCA Building in New York City

1957 — Dies in November

Focus: Reading for Understanding

1. Who was Diego Rivera's real teacher?

2. Rivera is credited for taking Europe in his stride. What was so unique about Rivera's talent and skill?

3. What is considered Rivera's greatest work?

4. Word Watch—Look up the following words and note how they are used in the article: *uncrating, enrich, reputation, clinch, scholarship, revolutionaries, hastened, syndicate,* and *ditching.*

Connect

1. This cover of TIME Magazine is a self-portrait of the famous painter Rivera. Draw your own self-portrait.

2. Rivera became talented in his interest with art. Make a list of your own talents and interests. Which of these can you work at to become better?

Explore

1. Locate a book in your school or public library that contains pictures of Rivera's artwork. Create a mural of your own.

2. Research other prominent artists. Compare and contrast their art with that of Rivera.

Jackie Robinson

TWENTY CENTS

TIME

THE WEEKLY NEWSMAGAZINE

JACKIE ROBINSON
He and the boss took a chance.
(Sport)

$6.00 A YEAR

Jackie Robinson

He shattered baseball's color barrier.

September 27, 1947

As part of TIME's special series on the 100 most important people of the twentieth century, legendary baseball player Hank Aaron shared his memories of Jackie Robinson in a 1999 essay, excerpted below. Aaron, who hit a record-breaking 755 home runs in the major league, was a teenager when Robinson appeared on TIME's cover in 1947.

I was 14 years old when I first saw Jackie Robinson. It was the spring of 1948, the year after Jackie changed my life by breaking baseball's color line. His team, the Brooklyn Dodgers, made a stop in my hometown of Mobile, Alabama, while barnstorming its way north to start the season. While he was there, Jackie spoke to a big crowd of black folks over on Davis Avenue. I think he talked about segregation, but I didn't hear a word that came out of his mouth. Jackie Robinson was such a hero to me that I couldn't do anything but gawk at him.

They say certain people are bigger than life, but Jackie Robinson is the only man I've known who truly was. In 1947, life in America—at least my America, and Jackie's—was segregation. It was two worlds that were afraid of each other. There were separate schools for blacks and whites, separate restaurants, separate hotels, separate drinking fountains, and separate baseball leagues. Life was unkind to black people who tried to bring those worlds together. It could be hateful. But Jackie Robinson, God bless him, was bigger than all of that.

Jackie Robinson had to be bigger than life. He had to be bigger than the Brooklyn teammates who got up a petition to keep him off the ball club, bigger than the pitchers who threw at him or the base runners who dug their spikes into his shin, bigger than the bench jockeys who hollered for him to carry their bags and shine their shoes, bigger than the so-called fans who mocked him with mops on their heads and wrote him death threats.

"There's never been another ballplayer who touched people as Jackie did."

To this day, I don't know how he withstood the things he did without lashing back. Somehow, Jackie had the strength to suppress his instincts, to sacrifice his pride for his people's. It was an incredible act of selflessness that brought the races closer together than ever before and shaped the dreams of an entire generation.

There's never been another ballplayer who touched people as Jackie did. Jackie was taking us over segregation's threshold into a new land whose scenery made every black person stop and stare in reverence. We were all with Jackie.

Jackie Robinson

Key Dates

1919 — Born in Cairo, Georgia, on January 31

1939 — UCLA football and track star

1942 — Enlists in the U.S. Army

1945 — Signs with Kansas City Monarchs Negro League; later signs with Brooklyn Dodgers farm team in Montreal

1947 — Begins playing for Dodgers

1949 — Wins National League's Most Valuable Player award

1972 — Dies in Stamford, Connecticut, on October 24

Focus: Reading for Understanding

1. What does it mean that Jackie Robinson broke baseball's "color line"? What did he endure in order to do so?

2. In 1947, in what ways was life in America segregated?

3. How does Hank Aaron view Robinson? Why does Aaron see Robinson as a hero?

4. Word Watch—Look up the following words and note how they are used in the article: *barnstorming, segregation, gawk, petition, hollered, mocked, withstood, lashing, suppress, selflessness, generation, threshold,* and *reverence.*

Connect

1. Think of someone you consider "bigger than life." Write a first-person narrative, like Aaron's, about him or her.

2. Read about Althea Gibson. Compare her experience to Robinson's. Discuss similarities and differences.

Explore

1. Are baseball teams today more racially balanced than in 1947? Pick a team and find out.

2. What happened to Robinson after 1947? Learn more about his later achievements.

Eleanor Roosevelt

TWENTY CENTS

TIME

THE WEEKLY NEWSMAGAZINE

ANNA ELEANOR ROOSEVELT

The scrambled world has superseded scrambled eggs.

(National Affairs)

Thos. D. McAvoy

$6.00 A YEAR

Eleanor Roosevelt

A First Lady with unequaled power

April 17, 1939

First Lady Eleanor Roosevelt is a woman of unequaled influence in the world, but unlike Cleopatra or Queen Elizabeth, her power is not that of a ruler. She is the wife of a ruler. But her power comes not from her influence on him, but from her influence on public opinion. It is a self-made influence, and it is unique for a woman to hold.

She was not afraid to speak out on a wide variety of controversial issues.

Six years ago, the tall, restless character who moved into the White House with Franklin Roosevelt was viewed by large portions of the American public with some degree of scorn if not alarm. They joked about her, calling her "Eleanor Everywhere." They couldn't believe that any one woman could sincerely embrace the number of interests she had in addition to being a wife, mother, and White House hostess.

Today, enough people have met Mrs. Roosevelt, talked with her at close range, and checked up on her to accept her for what she is. Everything she says, everything she does, is genuinely motivated. People who used to scoff now listen to her. They read with respect her books, magazine articles, and daily newspaper column. And, as her hold on her audience has grown, so have her skill and boldness in tackling subjects that, even three years ago, she would have avoided. In three years, the distribution of her column "My Day" has increased from 20 newspapers to 68, with a circulation of 4.5 million.

She used to write in safe, rounded phrases, using plenty of "howevers," noting exceptions and admitting alternatives. She made observations like, "It's a great life if you never get tired," and described her family's Sunday evening scrambled egg feasts.

Today, she still gives her readers a running account of her life's incredibly varied aspects. She writes about plays, pictures, people seen, babies patted, books read, weather experienced, letters received, and so on. But in the past six months, she has also come out forcefully on a wide variety of controversial issues. The scrambled world has replaced her family's Sunday evening scrambled egg feasts. Among the topics she has argued for: soil erosion control as an "investment," minimum-wage laws for farm workers and domestic laborers, and an end to racial discrimination.

In the privileged world where one can see anything, go anywhere, and get almost anything done, Eleanor Roosevelt wastes no chance to make up for long years of being (by her own account) a cloistered nobody. Since developing from a painfully shy, homely duckling into a self-confident swan of a woman with the nation for her pond, she has learned to sail through life with serenity.

Eleanor Roosevelt

Key Dates

1884 — Born in New York City on October 11

1905 — Marries distant cousin Franklin Delano Roosevelt

1932 — Franklin, crippled by polio since 1921, is elected president; Eleanor becomes his eyes and ears

1948 — Helps secure passage of the United Nations' Universal Declaration of Human Rights

1962 — Dies in New York City on November 7

Focus: Reading for Understanding

1. How did Eleanor Roosevelt develop from a "shy duckling" into a "self-confident swan"?

2. Why did people call the First Lady, "Eleanor Everywhere?" How and why did public opinion shift?

3. How did the "My Day" column change? What causes did Roosevelt champion?

4. Word Watch—Look up the following words and note how they are used in the article: *scorn, embrace, scoff, circulation, exceptions, alternatives, aspects, controversial, investment, minimum wage, domestic laborers, privileged, cloistered,* and *homely.*

Connect

1. Write one radio broadcast or "My Day" column as if you were First Lady today. What issues will you focus on?

2. Research Franklin D. Roosevelt's accomplishments as president. How were Eleanor Roosevelt's causes related to the challenges her husband faced?

Explore

1. Who is the first lady today? What is she known for? Find out more about and report on other notable first ladies and how they used their positions in the White House.

2. Read some of Roosevelt's columns or listen to her broadcasts.

Franklin Delano Roosevelt

TWENTY CENTS

TIME

THE WEEKLY NEWSMAGAZINE

MAN OF THE YEAR
This generation of Americans has indeed a rendezvous with destiny.

$5.00 A YEAR

Franklin Delano Roosevelt

He restored hope to America.

January 5, 1942

Franklin Roosevelt was TIME's "Man of the Year" in 1941. In 1999, TIME chose him as one of the three most influential people of the twentieth century, along with Einstein and Gandhi. An excerpt from the 1999 article appears below.

FDR believed that a democratic government had a responsibility to help Americans in distress.

Franklin Delano Roosevelt was president of the United States for 12 of the most tumultuous years in the life of the nation. He guided the nation through democracy's two monumental crises—the Great Depression and World War II.

"Men will thank God on their knees a hundred years from now that Franklin D. Roosevelt was in the White House," the New York Times wrote at the time of his death. "It was his leadership which inspired free men in every part of the world to fight with greater hope and courage."

Even through the grainy newsreels, we can see what the people at the time saw: the radiant smile, the eyes flashing with good humor, the good-natured toss of the head, the buoyant optimism, the confidence with which he met economic catastrophe and international crisis.

When Roosevelt assumed the presidency, America was in its third year of depression. No other decline in American history had been so deep, so lasting, so far reaching. Factories that had once produced steel, automobiles, furniture, and textiles stood eerily silent. One out of every four Americans was unemployed, and in the cities the number reached nearly 50%. In the countryside, crops that could not be sold at market rotted in the fields. More than half a million homeowners, unable to pay their mortgages, lost their homes and their farms; thousands of banks failed, destroying the life savings of millions. The federal government had virtually no mechanisms in place to provide relief.

Roosevelt believed that a democratic government had a responsibility to help Americans in distress—not as a matter of charity but as a matter of social duty. This conviction provided a moral compass to guide both his words and his actions. Roosevelt fashioned a New Deal, which fundamentally altered the relationship of the government to its people.

Massive public works projects put millions to work building schools, roads, and libraries. The Securities and Exchange Commission regulated a stock market that had been run as an insiders' game. Federal funds protected home mortgages; legislation guaranteed labor's right to organize and established minimum wages and maximum hours. And a sweeping Social Security system provided a measure of security and dignity to the elderly.

Franklin Delano Roosevelt

Key Dates

1882 — Born in Hyde Park, New York, on January 30

1921 — Contracts polio

1928–1932 — Serves as governor of New York

1932–1936 — Elected president; begins enacting New Deal legislation

1936–1940 — Reelected to office

1940–1944 — Elected to an unprecedented third term; United States enters World War II

1945 — Attends Yalta Conference; dies two months later on April 12

Focus: Reading for Understanding

1. What was happening in America when Franklin Roosevelt became president? What challenges did he face? How does the cover reflect this?

2. What role did Roosevelt believe government should play? Why does the writer call this Roosevelt's "moral compass"?

3. What did Roosevelt do to turn the country around?

4. Word Watch—Look up these words and note how they are used in the article: *distress, tumultuous, monumental, coalition, newsreels, buoyant, optimism, catastrophe, decline, eerily, mortgages, massive,* and *conservation.*

Connect

1. Compare the challenges of our president to those Roosevelt faced.

2. What do relatives or neighbors recall about the Great Depression, Roosevelt, and his New Deal programs?

Explore

1. The cover and the profile on Roosevelt are from two different issues of TIME. Research to find out Roosevelt's accomplishments as president. Do you think the impression of Roosevelt in 1942 was the same as it is in this 1999 article?

2. Who are the other men on this cover? Research to find out their names and their connection to Roosevelt.

Jonas Salk

Jonas Salk

He led the battle against polio.

March 29, 1954

In northern India's state of Uttar Pradesh last week, Muslim trappers working in teams of four set out their nets before dawn. While three hid, one man walked to a clump of trees. Loudly, he called "Ao! Ao! Ao!" ("Come! Come! Come!") and began to scatter grain. Rhesus monkeys scrambled down and followed his grain trail. When the monkeys got to the grain in the trap, a hidden operator pulled a cord and meshed them in the netting, an average of a dozen at a time.

Hordes of monkeys from India and the Philippines were used as ammunition in the great battle against polio.

The Muslims (no Hindu will do this work because of religious scruples) stuffed the monkeys into bamboo cages and carried them on shoulder poles into Lucknow. The train hauled them 260 miles to New Delhi. There, 1,000 specimens carefully chosen for health and size (4 to 8 lbs. each) were collected. Then, a four-engine transport flew them 4,000 miles to London. Next, another plane took them 3,000 miles to New York's Idlewild Airport. Then, trucks carried them 700 miles to Okatie Farms in South Carolina. There the rhesus monkeys from India were caged with other hordes of monkeys from the Philippines, to be used as ammunition in a great battle now being fought by medical science. The enemy: polio. These monkeys are used to research cures for polio.

The man behind most of this monkey business—the biggest in history—is Jonas Edward Salk, 39, an intense, single-minded medical researcher who spends his days and a large part of his nights in a laboratory at the University of Pittsburgh. Behind Salk, in turn, are 81 million of the 3 billion dimes that the U.S. public has given to the National Foundation for Infantile Paralysis.

This spring, Dr. Salk's vision and his delicate laboratory procedures are to be put to the test. Beginning next month in the South and working north ahead of the polio season, the vaccine that Salk has devised and concocted, will be shot into the arms of up to one-million youngsters in the first, second, and third grades in nearly 200 chosen test areas. A few months after the 1954 polio season is over, statisticians will dredge from a mountain of records an answer to the question: Does the Salk vaccine give effective protection against polio?

"This year's mass trials are the greatest gamble in medical history," says a polio researcher. If the Salk vaccine is effective for even one season, 1954 will be a year of victory against polio. If it is not, little will have been lost and much knowledge gained for a new attack.

Jonas Salk

Key Dates

1914 — Born in East Harlem, New York, on October 28

1939 — Graduates from New York University College of Medicine

1942 — Begins work on first commercial flu vaccine

1949 — Starts polio research with funding from the March of Dimes

1955 — Announces success of his polio vaccine and mass immunization begins

1995 — Dies at the age of 80

Focus: Reading for Understanding

1. What story does the cover tell? Why are the shots aimed at empty leg braces and crutches? What does "Is this the year?" mean?

2. Who was Jonas Salk? Why did he need to capture rhesus monkeys in India?

3. Word Watch—Look up these words and note how they are used in the article: *Muslims, Hindu, scruples, hordes, ammunition, single-minded, vaccine, devised, concocted, statisticians, dredge,* and *trials.*

Connect

1. When and how were you vaccinated against polio? What other vaccines have you had? What forms did they come in, and at what age did you have them? (Ask a parent or guardian to help you remember.)

2. Have a class debate about whether animals should be used for human medical research. Divide into two teams and brainstorm a list of pros and cons before you begin. Try to anticipate the other side's arguments.

Explore

Research the polio epidemic. Was Salk successful? Or, choose another major epidemic to research and report on to your class. Possibilities include smallpox, AIDS, mad-cow disease, the Ebola virus, or influenza.

Diana Spencer, Princess of Wales

SPECIAL REPORT

DIANA,
PRINCESS OF WALES

1961-1997

Diana Spencer, Princess of Wales

She was the people's princess.

September 8, 1997

On the day 16 years ago that Charles, the Prince of Wales, married Lady Diana Spencer, the Archbishop of Canterbury declared, here is "the stuff of which fairy tales are made." But, the princess also knew loneliness and heartbreak. The love story was false; it was shown, from the very beginning. The fairy tale ended in divorce. When it was over, Diana turned her attention to other causes that needed tending to—her sons, the sick, the war—ravaged, her own heart. The world watched her and held out the fragile hope of a happy-ever after ending for Diana. The marriage was dead, but long live the princess.

And now she is gone.

For 16 years, Diana in a sense stood for Britain, proving that despite the end of its empire and the weight of its history, the country was still capable of youth and energy and charm. By blood, she too, and not just Charles, was descended from James I, the first Stuart King. She was the first Englishwoman to marry an heir to the throne in more than 300 years. In Diana, the royal family had the warmest smile, the most soulful eyes. The public loved her.

As the princess who would become queen, Diana could turn the world's passion for her into compassion for others, whether they were the homeless, AIDS patients, or victims of land mines. Even after her marriage ended, the press still reported her every movement, every detail of her dress. But Diana knew how to use their interest in her for doing good. In an interview, she declared, "Being permanently in the public eye gives me a special responsibility—to use the impact of photographs to get a message across, to make the world aware of an important cause, to stand up for certain values."

> **Diana could turn the world's passion for her into compassion for others, whether they were the homeless, AIDS patients, or victims of land mines.**

Then one morning, Britain woke to find its darling dead, stolen away during the night as a result of a deadly car crash. Tony Blair, the British prime minister, on the way to a church service, was close to tears. Said he, "We are today a nation in a state of shock, in mourning, in grief that is so deeply painful for us. She was a wonderful and warm human being. Her own life was often sadly touched by tragedy, but she touched the lives of so many others in Britain and throughout the world with joy and comfort." He added, "She was the people's princess, and that is how she will stay in our hearts and memories forever."

Diana Spencer, Princess of Wales

Key Dates

1961 — Born in Sandringham, England on July 1

1981 — Marries Charles, the future king of England

1982 — Prince William born

1984 — Prince Harry born

1992 — Diana and Charles announce their separation

1993 — Diana reveals her plan to withdraw from public life

1996 — The divorce is finalized

1997 — Dies on August 31 after a car crash in Paris

Focus: Reading for Understanding

1. In what ways did Princess Diana Spencer's fairy tale turn into a tragedy?

2. What did Princess Diana feel were the responsibilities that came with her position? How did she use her role for the public good?

3. Why did Tony Blair call Diana the "people's princess"?

4. Word Watch—Look up the following words and note how they are used in the article: *heartbreak, war-ravaged, fragile, empire, descended, heir, passion, compassion, permanently, impact, mourning,* and *grief.*

Connect

1. What fairy tales about princesses do you know? Choose one and compare it to the "fairy tale" life of Princess Diana.

2. Find out about Queen Elizabeth, Hillary Rodham Clinton, and Eleanor Roosevelt. Compare the role of first lady to the roles of queen and princess.

Explore

The Royal Family is a source of great interest not only in Great Britain but in the United States. What is the family's role today? What challenges does it face?

Joseph Stalin

Joseph Stalin

He stopped Hitler from conquering Russia.

January 4, 1943

The year 1942 was a year of blood and strength. The man whose name means "steel" in Russian, whose few words of English include the American expression "tough guy," was the man of 1942. Only Joseph Stalin fully knew how close Russia stood to defeat in 1942, and only Joseph Stalin fully knew how he brought Russia through.

But the whole world knew what the alternative would have been. The man who knew it best of all was Adolf Hitler who found his past accomplishments turning into dust.

Had German soldiers swept past steel-stubborn Stalingrad and destroyed Russia's ability to fight back, Hitler would have been not only man of the year, but also the undisputed master of Europe, looking for other continents to conquer. He could have sent at least 250 victorious divisions to make new conquests in Asia and Africa. But Joseph Stalin stopped him. Stalin had done it before—in 1941—when he started with all of Russia intact. But Stalin's achievement of 1942 was far greater because his resources were far scarcer.

During 1941, Stalin had sold more than 400,000 miles of territory in order to save most of his army. Gone was nearly half of Russia's best farmland. Gone was a big fraction—how large only he knew—of the precious tanks, planes and war equipment.

Stalin had only one new resource in 1942: the help of the United States. But as events were to prove, that was to come late and to be bottlenecked by German attacks.

Had German soldiers taken over Stalingrad, Hitler would have been not only man of the year, but the undisputed master of Europe.

In his birch-paneled office within the dark-towered Kremlin, Joseph Stalin worked at his desk 16 to 18 hours a day. Before him he kept a huge globe showing the course of the fighting. There were new streaks of grey in his hair and new etchings of fatigue in his granite face. But there was no break in his hold on Russia.

To keep his home front intact, Stalin had only work and black bread to offer. He added a promise of victory in 1942 and called to his people to sacrifice collectively to preserve the things they had built collectively. Children and women foraged in forests for wood. Apartments went unheated. Electricity was turned off four days a week. At year's end, the Russian children had no new toys for the New Year's celebration. There was no smoked salmon, no goose, no vodka, no coffee for the grownups. But there was rejoicing. The Motherland had been saved for the second time in two years, and now victory and peace could not be too far off.

Joseph Stalin

Key Dates

1879 — Born on December 21

1922 — Becomes secretary general of the Communist Party

1928–1953 — Rules the Soviet Union with dictatorial force, ordering massive slaughter of his opponents

1939 — Signs "nonaggression pact" with Hitler

1941 — Stunned by Hitler's attack on Russia, Stalin eventually beats back German invasion and extends Communism to much of Eastern Europe

1953 — Dies on March 5 in Moscow

Focus: Reading for Understanding

1. What does Joseph Stalin's name mean in Russian? Why is this a fitting name for him?

2. What might have happened had Stalin not stopped Hitler?

3. What was Russia's situation in 1941?

4. What new resource did Stalin have in 1942?

5. Why was there rejoicing at New Year's in Russia in spite of the lack of food, heat, and electricity?

6. Word Watch—Look up the following words and note how they are used in the article: *alternative, undisputed, resources, scarcer, bottlenecked, fatigue, granite, intact, foraged, sacrifice, collectively,* and *preserve.*

Connect

Find out about Adolf Hitler and Mikhail Gorbachev. How are they similar to Stalin?

Explore

1. How did Russia get into and out of World War II?

2. Who was Karl Marx? What is Marxism? How did Stalin apply Marx's political ideas?

3. What is totalitarianism? In what ways did Stalin turn the Soviet Union into a totalitarian state?

Margaret Thatcher

Margaret Thatcher

The first woman to lead a major Western nation

May 14, 1979

Savor the moment. For the first time in history, two women were the main participants in Britain's traditional post-election ceremony. In this ritual, Britain's monarch invites the leader of the winning political party to Buckingham Palace and asks the leader to form a government. The monarch, of course, was Queen Elizabeth II. The prime minister was Margaret Hilda Thatcher, 53, a grocer's daughter from the English Midlands, who last week led her Conservative Party to a decisive victory over James Callaghan's Labor Party. The Tories won a solid majority of 43 seats in the 635-member House of Commons, and Thatcher thereby became not only the first woman to head a British government, but the first to lead a major Western nation.

Even before the vote established that the Conservatives had an absolute majority, outgoing Prime Minister Callaghan drove to Buckingham Palace last Friday to hand in his resignation to the Queen. Minutes later, Thatcher was on her way to "kiss hands" and receive the royal commission to form a government. Denis Thatcher accompanied his wife to the palace. Like prime ministers' spouses before him, he remained downstairs to chat with the Queen's aides.

Downing Street was packed with well-wishers and photographers when Thatcher arrived. Expressing delight and excitement over her victory, Britain's "Iron Lady" made a statement clearly addressed to a nation poised uneasily for change: "I would like to remember some words of St. Francis of Assisi, which I think are particularly apt at the moment: 'Where there is discord, may we bring harmony; where there is doubt, may we bring faith; where there is despair, may we bring hope.' Now that the election is over, may we get together and strive to serve and strengthen the country."

> **Thatcher takes her place alongside Israel's Golda Meir and India's Indira Gandhi as modern women politicians who have made it to the top.**

At Labor Party headquarters a few blocks away, "Sunny Jim" Callaghan, 67, spoke of his defeat with the same reserve and gentle dignity that marked his campaign. He publicly congratulated his successor as prime minister. "It is a great office," he said, "a wonderful privilege, and for a woman to occupy that office is, I think, a tremendous moment in the country's history. Therefore, everybody must, on behalf of all our people, wish her well and wish her success."

Thatcher thus takes her place alongside Israel's Golda Meir, India's Indira Gandhi, and Sri Lanka's Sirimavo Bandaranaike as modern women politicians who have made it to the top.

Margaret Thatcher

Key Dates

1925 — Born in Grantham, England, on October 13

1979 — Elected Britain's first female prime minister

1984 — Survives terrorist assassination attempt

1990 — Resigns after losing support of the Conservative Party over differences on European Community policy

1992 — Awarded title of Baroness Thatcher of Kesteven and takes seat in the House of Lords

Focus: Reading for Understanding

1. Describe the tradition of passing power from one person or party to the next after an election in England. What was so different in 1979?

2. Who is Jim Callaghan? What did he say about Margaret Thatcher's election?

3. What does the quotation by St. Francis of Assisi mean, and why do you think Thatcher chose it for this occasion?

4. Word Watch—Look up the following words and note how they are used in the article: *savor, monarch, decisive, majority, resignation, royal commission, spouses, apt, discord, despair, strive,* and *reserve.*

Connect

Find out about Golda Meir. Why is she mentioned in this article? Find Israel, India, England, and Sri Lanka on a world map. Which of these countries are considered "Western nations"?

Explore

What is 10 Downing Street? How is the role of prime minister different from the role of king or queen in England? Who is the prime minister in England today? Who is the king or queen? How do these roles compare to the role of president in the United States?

Harry S. Truman

Harry S. Truman
He ordered the dropping of the atomic bomb.

December 31, 1945

Nineteen forty-five was the year of the atom bomb. The world would remember the deadly mushroom clouds over Hiroshima and Nagasaki. Here were the force, the threat, the promise of the future. In their giant shadows, 45,000 feet tall, all men were infinitely small.

It was not a scientist who became, more than any other man, responsible for the bomb's use in 1945 and its future. It was an ordinary man, of average size and weight, wearing bifocal glasses, fond of plain food and lodge meetings. It was Harry Truman, 32nd president of the United States.

Harry Truman had never dreamed of being Man of the Atomic Year.

In the 1920s, Harry Truman was content to be an obscure Missouri county judge. In the 1930s, by the chance whim of a political boss, he found himself in the U.S. Senate. As 1945 began, he was vice president, a man struck by political lightning at the Chicago convention while eating a hotdog with mustard.

As the year started, Harry Truman had no idea that his government was engaged in atomic research. At year's end, President Truman was the man in charge of the bomb and its precarious secret.

Harry Truman, a very plain man indeed, had never sought or dreamed of being Man of the Atomic Year. Like most of mankind, he was not prepared for the destiny and the responsibility that had been thrust upon him.

When the bomb was dropped, by his order, on Hiroshima, Truman was aboard the cruiser Augusta, returning from his first international conference. He rushed to the officers' wardroom and announced breathlessly: "Keep your seats, gentlemen …We have just dropped a bomb on Japan which has more power than 20,000 tons of TNT. It was an overwhelming success." Applause and cheering broke out.

His formal announcement, released at the White House, showed considerably more awareness of what the bomb meant to humanity in good and evil.

Truman announced that the United States intended to keep the secret of the bomb to itself. But other nations would not accept this. The Germans had started the race for the bomb; the Japanese had been experimenting, too. Now, the Russians started working furiously. Scientists announced that in three to five years, any nation could learn the bomb's secret.

There was as yet no sign of confidence from the "Man of the Year," nor from most of humanity, that anything could be done about the problem. The feeling was abroad that the complexity of modern life had made all men, even presidents, mere flecks of foam on the tide.

Harry S. Truman

Key Dates

1884 — Born in Lamar, Missouri, on May 8

1918 — Serves in France during World War I

1934 — Elected to Senate from Missouri

1945 — Succeeds Roosevelt as president after three months as vice president

1948 — Defeats Thomas Dewey in race for president

1972 — Dies in Kansas City, Missouri, on December 26

Focus: Reading for Understanding

1. How is Harry Truman portrayed in this article? Explain the symbolism on the cover.

2. How did Truman's first announcement about dropping the bomb differ from his second?

3. Why was it important for America to try to keep the secret of the atom bomb? How did other nations react?

4. Word Watch—Look up the following words and note how they are used in the article: *infinitely, bifocal, obscure, whim, political boss, precarious, wardroom, complexity, mere,* and *flecks.*

Connect

1. How do you feel about the use of nuclear weapons? If you were president, could you order the dropping of an atomic bomb?

2. Americans learn about the end of World War II from an American perspective. How might the story differ for students in Japan? For Japanese Americans? Discuss.

Explore

1. Find a picture of the mushroom cloud. How did Japan's leaders respond to the dropping of the bomb?

2. What effects did the bomb have on Japan's people and land?

Lech Walesa

Lech Walesa

"He gave us hope."

December 29, 1980

In the modestly furnished living room of a Gdansk apartment, the little man with a flowing reddish-brown mustache chain-smokes Polish cigarettes as he chats with a group of visitors. Six months ago, Lech Walesa (pronounced Vah-wen-sah) was an unemployed electrician. Today, as leader of the Communist world's only independent labor union (Solidarity), he is one of the most powerful men in Poland. He is a folk hero not only to millions of his countrymen but to much of the world. His achievement all but defies description. In effect, he single-handedly rallied his fellow workers to stand up against the will and might of the Soviet Union.

Walesa looks ill-suited for such eminence. Yet he radiates an unmistakable air of authority, along with an infectious good humor. Working a crowd, he displays the charisma of a natural leader. Said a Gdansk woman after hearing him speak last week: "He is the right man at the right time. He was able to give us hope."

Poland poses the gravest threat to the Soviet Union. Events there have stripped the clothes right off the empire. Walesa and his colleagues in the Solidarity leadership know that they are, as it were, condemned to Communism; their basic goal is not to reject the system but to make it work better. However, the workers' revolt shouts out Communism's economic and ideological failures and reminds the world that the glue of Soviet influence is force and intimidation, not shared purpose. The Polish challenge comes from the workers—the only class of which the Soviet Union is afraid.

> ## "He is the right man at the right time. He was able to give us hope."

The formation of Poland's independent trade unions attacked the heart of Communist Party theology—that it is the sole authentic representative of the working class. It's in trouble if it cannot command its own workers. For this reason, the Soviets are nervous that the Polish disease will catch elsewhere in the Soviet's East bloc and touch off workers demands for free unions and other liberalizations.

By comparison with other East bloc nations, Polish life is seemingly not all that bad. The average wage ($200 per month) and per capita meat consumption are surpassed only in East Germany and Czechoslovakia. Private bank accounts are legal, passports easy to obtain, and the state provides the usual Communist benefits: free medical care, guaranteed jobs. But this was not enough. Poles were tired of standing in endless lines; tired of shoddy, overpriced goods; and tired of waiting eight to ten years for an apartment. As a striking worker put it last August, "We don't want to run the government. We just want a decent life."

Lech Walesa

Key Dates

1943 — Born on September 29 in Popowo, Poland

1978 — Organizes first free trade union in Poland

1980 — Leads Gdansk shipyard strike; becomes leader of Solidarity

1981 — Arrested; named TIME's "Man of the Year"

1982 — Released from internment

1983 — Awarded Nobel Peace Prize; martial law is lifted

1989 — Solidarity legalized; becomes third person ever to address a joint session of the U.S. Congress

1990 — Elected president in Poland

1995 — Defeated for second term

Focus: Reading for Understanding

1. What was Lech Walesa able to accomplish for the Polish people?

2. What characteristics does Walesa have that attracted people to him?

3. What was formed in Poland that attacked the heart of the Communist Party theory?

4. Word Watch—Look up the following words and note how they are used in the article: *shoddy, defies, ill-suited, infectious, single-handedly, rallied, eminence, gravest,* and *authentic.*

Connect

1. At the time of this article, a "cold war" was taking place. Ask neighbors and family members what it was like to live during the cold war.

2. Read about Nelson Mandela. Compare and contrast these two leaders.

Explore

1. What is Communism? What are some of the benefits that one receives in a Communist country? Is Poland a Communist country today?

2. Locate Poland on a map. What is this country known for, in terms of trade, tourism, and natural resources?

Oprah Winfrey

OCTOBER 5, 1998 $2.95

www.time.com

STARR: TRIPPED UP?
HEROES FOR THE PLANET

TIME

The most successful woman on TV fulfills a dream by returning to movies in a story about slavery, passion and family. An exclusive visit with...

The Beloved Oprah

Oprah Winfrey
Bewitching Beloved

October 5, 1998

"Thin love ain't no love at all," says Sethe, the fiercely defiant runaway slave in Toni Morrison's novel *Beloved*. Oprah Winfrey's love for the book was thick, warm, abiding. With eyewitness immediacy and her view of fictive art, Morrison brought the intimate evil of slavery to life in the story of a mother's ultimate sacrifice. When Winfrey discovered the novel upon its publication in 1987, she was moved as a reader, as an African American, and as a woman who suffered the death of the child she gave birth to when she was fourteen. For Oprah, *Beloved* was a central fable of her race and her sex. She knew she had to produce a movie version, and she meant to cast herself in the lead role.

What Oprah wants, Oprah gets. She has, after all, earned an Oscar nomination for her first movie part in Steven Spielberg's *The Color Purple*. For more than a decade, she has dominated the afternoon airwaves with her syndicated talk show. She is among the nation's most admired and influential people.

Achievement seems to follow Oprah wherever she goes. At the age of 19, Oprah was the youngest person and the first African American to anchor the news at a television station in Nashville, Tennessee. Oprah has won numerous awards, including nine Emmy Awards for Outstanding Talk Show. She is also one of three women, including Lucille Ball and Mary Pickford, to own a television studio. Her current talk show, *The Oprah Winfrey Show*, is the highest-rated television talk show in television history. In June of 1998, Oprah was named one of the 100 most-influential people of the twentieth century by TIME Magazine.

She is among the nation's most admired and influential people.

This same passion and drive has extended to other areas of influence. Oprah has brought attention to many areas with her philanthropic efforts. In 1997, Oprah began the Oprah's Angel Network, which has collected millions of dollars in spare change to use as donations. Oprah has donated the money to higher-education institutions, set up scholarship funds for many individuals, and serves as a spokesperson for an organization that gives inner-city school children a chance to attend many of the nation's finest schools. Oprah's interest in reading and literacy has called attention to the importance of reading and books. Oprah also testified before Congress to support the enactment of the National Child Protection Act, which was signed into law by President Clinton in 1993.

Oprah Winfrey

Key Dates

1954 — Born in Kosciusko, Mississippi on January 29

1973 — Becomes the first African American to anchor the news at Nashville's WTVF-TV

1984 — Becomes host of *A.M. Chicago*

1985 — Nominated for Academy Award for best supporting actress in *The Color Purple*

1986 — Begins *The Oprah Winfrey Show* and sets up own production company

1993 — President Clinton signs the "Oprah Bill" which aims to protect children

Focus: Reading for Understanding

1. Besides Oprah Winfrey, who are the only two women to have owned their own television studios?

2. For what did Winfrey receive an Oscar nomination?

3. To which causes has Winfrey donated time and money?

4. Word Watch—Look up the following words and note how they are used in the article: *philanthropic, defiant, abiding, most-influential, airwaves, enactment, fiercely,* and *studio.*

Connect

Winfrey has donated millions of dollars and her time to a variety of causes. Which causes are you interested in and willing to donate time? Determine a plan. Make arrangements to be a volunteer in your community. Share your experience with the class.

Explore

1. Winfrey was named one of the most influential people of the twentieth century by TIME Magazine. Who are some of the other people on that list? Are any of those individuals in this collection of famous faces?

2. Research the National Child Protection Act. What does this law do?

Orville Wright

Orville Wright

With his brother, he pioneered human flight.

December 3, 1928

A biting cold wind was blowing 24 miles an hour along the beach at Kitty Hawk, North Carolina, on the morning of December 17, 1903. The Wright brothers, with their biplane and a few helpers, were on a hill. Dismally nearby was a horse and wagon. A man sat on the wagon seat, the reins looped over a crooked finger. He was an undertaker.

The Wrights' first flight lasted 12 seconds and covered 120 feet of ground.

The plane resembled a great, wide box kite. The engine was at one side of the flyer's seat, so that if the plane tumbled, it would not fall on him. Two skids projected in front to prevent the plane from somersaulting when it landed.

As boys in Dayton, Ohio, the Wright brothers played with kites and gliders and became expert in flying them. When they were young men, they worked in the bicycle business and continued to study aerodynamics. They learned how to shape the wings of a plane, how to steer it, how to control it in all ways. They built their own motor. And then, they were ready to make their first flight.

At Kitty Hawk that cold December week, Wilbur and Orville Wright tossed a coin to decide who would try the first flight. Wilbur won, got into the machine, and rose a few feet. After three seconds, the machine stalled. Next, it was Orville's turn. He succeeded.

Orville's first flight lasted 12 seconds and covered 120 feet of ground.

In 1903, most Americans found it hard to believe that flying would ever become a popular means of transportation. So, the Wrights went to Europe. There, they won recognition and financial backing.

Soon, Orville and Wilbur Wright, who never attended college, received honorary academic degrees. And, of course, they made money. In 1915, three years after Wilbur Wright's death, Orville sold his patents to the Wright Aeronautical Corp. It is a $7 million business.

Now, at 57, Orville lives in Dayton, Ohio, working at aeronautical research.

During the 25 years since the Wrights' first flight, various planes have crossed the Atlantic, Pacific, and Arctic oceans. They have risen to 38,418 feet, stayed in the air 65 hours and 25 minutes, traveled 4,466 miles without stopping, and sped 319 miles per hour. They have crossed North America from the Pacific, to the Atlantic in 18 hours and 58 minutes, and from the Atlantic to the Pacific in 24 hours and 51 minutes.

Passenger, express, and mail planes now cover 20,327 miles of routes. To travel by air costs on the average three times as much as by rail.

Orville Wright

Key Dates

1867 — Wilbur born in Millville, Indiana, on April 16

1871 — Orville born in Dayton, Ohio, on August 19

1899–1902 — The brothers build and test kites and gliders

1903 — The brothers' first successful flight at Kitty Hawk

1906 — Wrights establish patents on airplane-control system

1912 — Wilbur dies of typhoid

1915 — Orville sells airplane factory

1948 — Orville dies of a heart attack

Focus: Reading for Understanding

1. Why was an undertaker waiting at Kitty Hawk? What other precautions did the Wright brothers take before their historic flight?

2. This article was written on the 25th anniversary of the Wright brothers' flight. How did transportation and public attitudes toward transportation change between 1903 and 1928?

3. Word Watch—Look up the following words and note how they are used in the article: *dismally, undertaker, skids, aerodynamics, stalled, honorary degrees, patents,* and *aeronautical.*

Connect

1. Read the profile of another TIME person. How are these stories related?

2. Make a model of the Wright brothers' plane. What principles enable the brothers' plane to fly?

Explore

1. Trace the history of commercial aviation post-Wright brothers.

2. What do you imagine will be the next mode of public transportation in the future? Brainstorm, then draw a picture or create an advertisement for your imagined mode of transport.

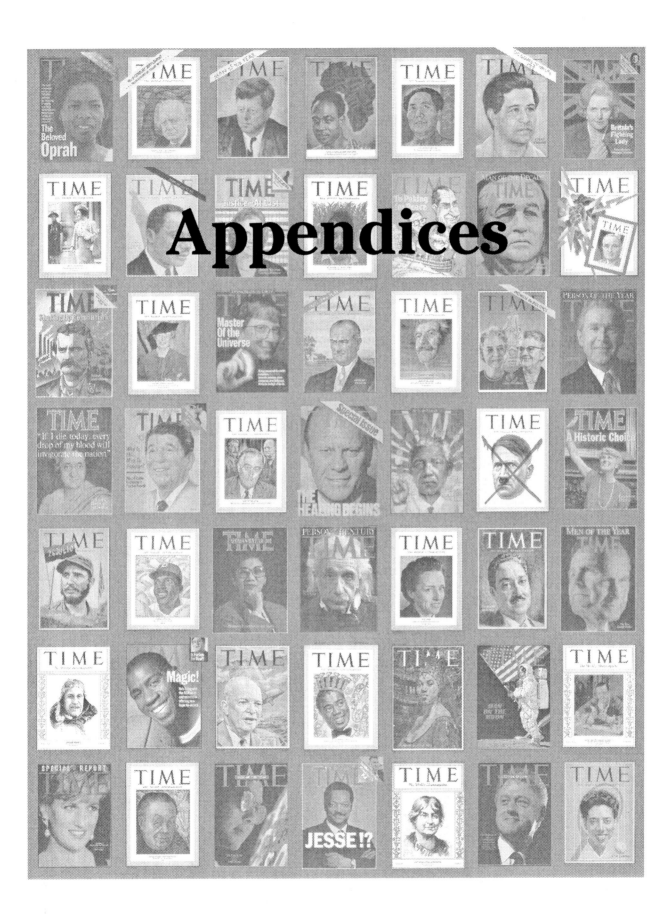

Appendices

References Cited

Barton, Keith, and Linda Levstik. 2004. *History for the common good*. London: Lawrence Erlbaum.

Donaldson, Margaret. 1986. *Children's minds*. New York: HarperCollins Publishers Ltd.

Gardner, Howard. 1983. *Frames of mind: The theory of multiple intelligences*. New York: Basic Books.

Jackson, Kenneth. T, 1989. A special issue: The Bradley Commission on history in the schools. *The History Teacher* 23:73–78.

Mullins, Sandra L. 1990. Social studies for the 21st Century: Recommendations of the national commission on social studies in the schools. ERIC Clearinghouse for Social Studies/Social Science Education Bloomington, IN. ERIC ED329484.

Teele, Sue. 1994. Redesigning the educational system to enable all students to succeed. Doctoral dissertation, University of California—Riverside.

Turner, Thomas. 2003. *Essentials of elementary social studies*. Boston: Allyn & Bacon.

Wilson, Virginia, James Litle, and Gerald Lee Wilson. 1993. *Teaching social studies: Handbook of trends, issues and implications for the future*. Connecticut: Greenwood Publishing Group.

Contents of the Teacher Resource CD

Page Number	Name	Filename
79	Madeleine Albright	albright.jpg
82	Corazon Aquino	aquino.jpg
85	Louis Armstrong	armstrg1.jpg
88	Neil Armstrong	armstrg2.jpg
91	Menachem Begin and Anwar Sadat	bgnsdt.jpg
94	Queen Elizabeth Bowes-Lyon	bowesln.jpg
97	George H. W. Bush	bush1.jpg
100	George W. Bush	bush2.jpg
103	Jimmy Carter	carter.jpg
106	Fidel Castro	castro.jpg
109	Carrie Chapman Catt	catt.jpg
112	Cesar Chavez	chavez.jpg
115	Winston Churchill	churchil.jpg
118	Bill Clinton	clinton1.jpg
121	Hillary Rodham Clinton	clinton2.jpg
124	Margaret Chase Smith and Lucia Cormier	corsmith.jpg
127	Eve Curie	curie.jpg
130	Walt Disney	disney.jpg
133	Thomas Edison	edison.jpg
136	Albert Einstein	einstein.jpg
139	Dwight Eisenhower	eisenhwr.jpg
142	Geraldine Ferraro	ferraro.jpg
145	Gerald Ford	ford1.jpg
148	Henry Ford	ford2.jpg
151	Aretha Franklin	franklin.jpg
154	Indira Gandhi	gandhi1.jpg
157	Mohandas Gandhi	gandhi2.jpg
160	Bill Gates	gates.jpg
163	Althea Gibson	gibson.jpg
166	Mikhail Gorbachev	gorbachv.jpg

Contents of the Teacher Resource CD *(cont.)*

Page Number	Name	Filename
169	Alex Haley	haley.jpg
172	Adolf Hitler	hitler.jpg
175	David Ho	ho.jpg
178	Jesse Jackson	jackson.jpg
181	Lyndon B. Johnson	johnson.jpg
184	John F. Kennedy	kennedy.jpg
187	Martin Luther King Jr.	king.jpg
190	Nelson Mandela	mandela.jpg
193	Mao Zedong	mao.jpg
196	Thurgood Marshall	marshall.jpg
199	Golda Meir	meir.jpg
202	Maria Montessori	montesri.jpg
205	Mother Teresa	mother.jpg
208	Richard Nixon	nixon.jpg
211	Kwame Nkrumah	nkrumah.jpg
214	Sandra Day O'Connor	oconnor.jpg
217	Eva Perón	peron.jpg
220	Ronald Reagan	reagan.jpg
223	Diego Rivera	rivera.jpg
226	Jackie Robinson	robinson.jpg
229	Eleanor Roosevelt	rosevlt1.jpg
232	Franklin Delano Roosevelt	rosevlt2.jpg
235	Jonas Salk	salk.jpg
238	Diana Spencer, Princess of Wales	spencer.jpg
241	Joseph Stalin	stalin.jpg
244	Margaret Thatcher	thatcher.jpg
247	Harry S. Truman	truman.jpg
250	Lech Walesa	walesa.jpg
253	Oprah Winfrey	winfrey.jpg
256	Orville Wright	wright.jpg

Notes

Notes

264